Fast-Forward

YOUR QUILTING

A New Approach to Quick Piecing

DINA PAPPAS

Martingale®
& COMPANY

CREDITS

President • *Nancy J. Martin*
CEO • *Daniel J. Martin*
Publisher • *Jane Hamada*
Editorial Director • *Mary V. Green*
Managing Editor • *Tina Cook*
Technical Editor • *Cyndi Hershey*
Copy Editor • *Ellen Balstad*
Design Director • *Stan Green*
Illustrator • *Laurel Strand*
Cover & Text Designer • *Trina Stahl*
Photographer • *Brent Kane*

That Patchwork Place® is an imprint of
Martingale & Company®.

Fast-Forward Your Quilting: A New Approach to
Quick Piecing
© 2004 by Dina Pappas

Martingale & Company
20205 144th Avenue NE
Woodinville, WA 98072-8478 USA
www.martingale-pub.com

Printed in China
09 08 07 06 05 04   8 7 6 5 4 3 2 1

MISSION STATEMENT

*Dedicated to providing quality products and service
to inspire creativity.*

Library of Congress Cataloging-in-Publication Data

Pappas, Dina.
    Fast-forward your quilting / Dina Pappas.
      p. cm.
    ISBN 1-56477-508-9
    1. Patchwork—Patterns. 2. Quilting—Patterns. I. Title.
    TT835 .P3518 2004
    746 . 46'041—dc22

                                    2003016630

DEDICATION

To Marguerita McManus, for all your encouragement to think big and for your help with the
brainstorming.

ACKNOWLEDGMENTS

I would like to thank the following people:
    My husband, Jim Pappas, for his help
handling the details.
    Mary LaTour, Marguerita McManus, Deb
Cadwallender, and Judy Bolechala, for their
assistance with the quilts, which helped me meet
the deadline.
    Kathy Seal and her Thimbleberries Club,
for the opportunity to speak, which sparked the
idea for this book.
    Tina Schwager, at Freudenburg Non-
wovens, Pellon Consumer Products Division,
for so generously keeping me in interfacing
and for developing such a versatile line of interfacings.
    Susan Neill and Benartex, for those yummy
Fossil Fern swatches that I love to work with.
    Faye Burgos and Marcus Brothers, for their
encouragement and generous supply of the
vibrant fabrics for "Hothouse Tulips."
    And Martingale & Company. Their won-
derful team always produces beautiful books that
allow me to present my ideas.

⇒ *Contents* ⇐

Introduction

Let me introduce you to a fast way to accurately piece quilts. With gridded fusible interfacing, you can sew up to 85% fewer seams than you would with traditional piecing methods. Just like pushing the fast-forward button on a remote control, this method will fast-forward your quilting.

Traditional piecing methods require quilters to stitch blocks, then join the blocks into rows, and then join the rows to make the quilt top. Fast-forward quilting combines these steps. You simply fuse units onto gridded interfacing and *then* stitch the seams. You get the same job done with a lot less stitching.

All of the projects in this book could be stitched traditionally, but since the fast-forward method saves so much time and effort, why would you want to? As I wrote the book, I calculated how many seams I would have stitched if I'd used traditional methods rather than fast-forward piecing. On every quilt, especially the queen-size quilts, the number of seams I stitched was about one-tenth of those required by traditional methods.

Both experienced and beginning quilters have an "aha" moment when they realize that they can speed up piecing by using fusible interfacing. I received a wildly popular response to my books *Quick Watercolor Quilts* and *More Quick Watercolor Quilts*, both of which focus on piecing with fusible interfacing. When I teach the fusible watercolor method, people often ask if the same techniques could be used for traditional quilts. I always answer, "Absolutely!"

Fast-Forward Your Quilting will guide you through all the steps needed to successfully use the fusible technique. We'll discuss tools, fabric selection, and finishing techniques. Instructions for cutting and sewing a variety of basic units will give you a firm foundation on which to build your own blocks. Then I'll show you how to fuse your units onto a gridded interfacing foundation so that you can get accurate results—even if your piecing isn't!

Everything from choosing blocks to calculating interfacing yardage is covered. Easy-to-use charts will help you calculate the amount of interfacing needed for any project, whether it's set straight or on-point.

Once we've laid the groundwork, we'll explore twelve projects made with basic units. You'll see a variety of settings and sashings, and you'll learn tricks for adding pieced borders with the fast-forward method. Along the way, look for the fast-forward symbol ❯❯❯ . This symbol will lead you to tips for success and let you know it's time to hang on as you speed up your quilting.

Please join me, whatever your skill level, and let's fast-forward your quilting.

—Dina

Supplies

The following items will help you fast-forward your quilting.

Interfacing: Lightweight, gridded fusible interfacing makes the fuse, fold, and stitch method possible. It's readily available in most fabric stores and well-stocked quilt shops. It comes in a variety of widths, including 22", 44", and 48". Printed grid sizes come in 1", 1½", and 2" squares and can be found in straight-set and on-point grids. See "Fast-Forward Quilting with Interfacing" on page 10 to learn how to choose the best grid size for your project. Whatever the grid dimensions and layout, make sure the interfacing is fusible. Some preprinted grid materials are not fusible. Check with your fingers for the bumpy dots (the glue); they are what secure the fabric to the interfacing.

It is important that the fabric pieces fuse securely to the interfacing grid; however, you also want to add as little bulk as possible. I use lightweight fusible interfacing regardless of what type of fabrics I'm using in my quilt. Lightweight interfacing works great with cotton, but if you use heavier fabrics you may have to re-press occasionally, because they tend to come unfused.

Batting: Choosing a batting for your quilt is a personal decision. Since I enjoy doing lots of quilting on my interfaced quilts, I prefer a thin, low-loft batting to make quilting easier. With thinner batting, there is less bulk to fit under the machine.

Thread: For piecing, use thread suitable for machine sewing and choose a thread color that blends with the fabrics you are stitching. For machine quilting, use a quality machine-sewing thread that accents the quilt top. This is your opportunity to add color, sheen, and texture. Thread can be very exciting! For hand quilting, use specially designated hand-quilting thread in a suitable color.

Sewing Machine: Most straight-stitch sewing machines work well for the projects in this book. Having the right presser foot can make your sewing experience more enjoyable. If the following feet didn't come with your sewing machine, look for them at a quilt shop or sewing-machine service center.

Walking foot with guide bar: This attachment feeds multiple layers of fabric through the machine at the same rate, helping to prevent puckering. Also called an even-feed foot, it "walks" over the top layer of fabric as the feed dogs pull the bottom layer along. It is used for straight-line quilting and attaching binding, and it is useful in piecing bulky seams.

Free-motion quilting foot, also called a darning foot: This has a spring or a bar that fits over the screw holding the needle. The foot holds the fabric down as the stitch is made, and then the foot releases the fabric, allowing you to move the quilt sandwich when quilting.

Remember to treat your machine well by replacing the needle after each project and cleaning the lint from your machine. Also occasionally oil the machine according to the manufacturer's instructions.

Rotary Cutter and Mat: The rotary cutter is an essential tool for accurate, fast cutting. Keep fresh blades and change yours often for a "hot knife through butter" cutting experience. The cutting mat often doubles as my design area. I like a large mat, 23" x 35", which gives me room to square up panels and cut multiple fabric strips.

Rulers: For an accurate cut, you need a clear acrylic ruler to guide the rotary blade. Choose a 24" ruler for general strip cutting and squaring up quilt tops. A 6" square ruler is nice for squaring up units and trimming points. Look for rulers that have 45°-angle lines to use when mitering borders or trimming pieces at an angle.

Reducing Glass: A reducing glass looks like a magnifying glass, but it shrinks an image rather than enlarging it. You can get the same results by looking through the view-finder of a camera. A door peephole, available in some quilt shops or hardware stores, works to give an even smaller view. By looking at a design through a reducing glass or from a distance, you gain a new perspective. It allows you to see the overall effect of the design, secondary patterns, color balance, and any problem areas. I find these tools very valuable.

Ruby Beholder®: The Ruby Beholder is a red acrylic bar with a view finder at one end. Use the red acrylic portion to help determine a fabric's value; that is, its relative lightness or darkness. When you look at a group of fabrics through the red bar, the red acts as a filter, screening out the distraction of color to let you see value instead—light or medium or dark. The Ruby Beholder is a wonderful tool, but note that it won't work with red fabrics. For red fabrics you can use a piece of green-tinted plastic, such as a green plastic file folder.

You can also use a Ruby Beholder to check the diagonal seam lines of tall triangle units. See "Tall Triangles" on page 31 for more detailed information.

Irons and Ironing Boards: Miniature irons are useful for basting units in place on the interfacing grid. Once you line up any seam lines, you can baste the units by fusing the seam lines with the iron.

You need a clean, standard-size iron for fusing and pressing seams. The glue of fusible interfacing can leave residue on your iron so be careful to keep the iron off the interfacing as you press. Keep the soleplate clean to prevent residue from transferring onto your quilt.

If your ironing board is adjustable, raise it to the height of your worktable and butt the two together. You will increase your design space, and you'll be able to slide your work onto the ironing board without disturbing the layout. Portable pressing mats also allow you to press at your work space.

Quilting Gloves: Quilting gloves with little gripper dots on the palm side allow you to grip interfacing panels and control the quilt sandwich with less pressure from your hands. They're especially nice when you are machine quilting a large project because they lessen the stress on your back and neck.

Alcohol Wipes: Keep a few alcohol wipes on hand to remove any adhesive residue buildup on your sewing table. Fusible interfacing can leave a slightly sticky residue that tends to transfer to the sewing table and keep the interfacing panel from feeding smoothly through the machine.

Plastic Scouring Pad: If the interfacing becomes fused to the ironing board instead of to the fabric, a scouring pad will help remove the fusible residue. They are also handy for sweeping up threads, clipped dog-ears, and fabric snippets from the cutting mat and ironing board.

Fabric Selection

I prefer to use 100%-cotton fabrics for quiltmaking, but since your fast-forward quilt will be stabilized by an interfacing foundation, you can also use other fabrics normally considered too bulky or fragile for quilts. Even flannel, silk, and decorator fabrics can be used with this technique.

With so many beautiful fabrics available, choosing just a few for a particular quilt can be a challenge. As you develop your color skills, trust your instincts on what appeals to you. You know beauty when you see it.

Often quilters have a particular use or location in mind for a planned project, such as hanging it in a room that has a set color scheme. Use this color scheme as your starting point. Next, find fabrics that work with that color scheme.

Other color-scheme ideas might originate with a piece of art, a photo, or a wallpaper pattern you like. A decorating theme such as an Asian or country look can also guide print and color selections.

Many quilters like to start with a focus fabric. Focus fabrics, also known as theme fabrics, are medium- to large-scale prints and are usually multicolored. Generally speaking, they are the type of fabric that catches your eye and calls to you! They are usually the fabrics that you just love.

Find a focus fabric you like and study the colors within it. Some fabrics have color dots printed on the selvages. The dots indicate the number of screens used to print the fabric. Use those dots to help you find fabrics with similar colors. Focus fabrics are wonderful to use anywhere in a quilt and especially as an outer border. Using a focus fabric in that position helps give the quilt a cohesive look. Accumulate fabrics, including a background(s), within the focus fabric range of colors. Do you have a variety of textures, values, and a fabric that

Two-color quilts are tried-and-true winners. In this assortment of fabrics, the dominant impression is of red and white, but notice that there are a variety of prints. They differ in style and scale, which adds visual interest. A few multicolored prints add variety without weakening the overall impression of a simple two-color combination.

Asian Focus Fabric, Coordinates, and a Bright Fabric That "Sparkles" or Adds Life

"sparkles" or adds life? If the group of fabrics seems dull, try adding a punch with a fabric that is just a bit different from the others in color or texture. On the bolt, these punchy fabrics may scream "obnoxious" yet in the final quilt they can add that "wow" factor.

Pile your choices on the cutting table and step back. Do you love them, hate them, or notice one that just doesn't work? Trust your judgment now. If you have a nagging feeling that the combination isn't quite right, ask the shop employees for an opinion. They may suggest a substitute fabric with a different texture, scale, or color that you hadn't considered. Try it and repeat your evaluation. Again, trust your own judgment while being willing to stretch a bit.

> >> Instead of lugging bolts around a shop, look in the fat-quarter area and quickly pull several fabric choices. Mix and match fabric combinations until you're satisfied. Then, go to the shelves and find the same fabrics on the bolts. Armed with a stack of fat quarters, you may want to hold your choices against the fabric bolts to see what else is in your desired color range. You may be surprised to find another large print or floral within your color scheme to add to the mix.

Eliminate fabrics that do the same job—those that are the same shade and texture. Be sure to include a variety of textures (monochromatic prints, small-scale prints, medium-scale prints), values (lights, mediums, and darks), and a sparkle fabric. While you may use only one sparkle fabric, it can be enough to add some life to the final quilt.

Look at that pile! Your next question is how much fabric to buy. If you're making a pattern from this book and know which fabric will go in each position, the answer is easy—follow the yardage list in the project instructions. If you want to achieve a scrappy look instead of using the same fabric for a certain position, match the number of fabrics to the number of strips needed of that color. Buy yardage to equal the required total. If you don't have a specific project in mind or don't know the fabric position within a project, I recommend buying at least 1- to 2-yard pieces of background fabrics, ½- to 1-yard pieces of blenders, and ¼- to ½-yard pieces of sparkle fabrics. Buy larger amounts of those fabrics you love and may want to use for borders.

What if you find that you didn't buy enough? You can always add more fabrics if needed, substituting a similar shade or texture if you can't find or don't want an exact match. Adding more fabrics in a variety of shades and textures can very interesting and visually stimulating. Live on the edge by adding one fabric that is daring for you! If you hate the final combination, take it out before you fuse the design in place.

AUDITION THE FABRICS FOR THEIR ROLE

If you haven't followed a specific yardage list to buy your fabrics, you may still be unsure how to use the fabrics to their best advantage. I couldn't make up my mind regarding where to use the fabrics in "Vintage Memories" on page 65, which is based on a scrappy look, so I cut small scraps of the fabrics, printed a copy of the blocks, and then tried the fabrics in different positions within the block. When I found a combination that I liked, I glued the fabrics in place on the photocopy. Next, using different fabrics, I repeated the formula I discovered. I placed dark fabrics, floral fabrics, and light fabrics in similar places on each arm of one star. When I was ready to lay the units on interfacing, I had a guide for the fabric positions and combinations in each star. When the entire quilt was laid out on interfacing, I finalized my fabric choices and changed a few star centers to improve the color combination. I provide a quilt plan (master design) for each project in this book. You may find this plan quite helpful as you formulate your ideas and audition fabrics.

was actually quite dark when compared to the other medium-value fabrics. A Ruby Beholder can also be useful in determining value.

Auditioning Fabrics

Checking Value

To successfully use many fabrics in combinatin, audition them by their value. With "Water Lilies" on page 38, I assigned each piece of the block a value—dark tips, floral petals, light buds, and medium bases. I then created four fabric combinations. I checked all of the fabrics together to see if I had achieved a pleasing color and value combination. Then I grouped the fabrics by value to see if the piles of light, medium, and dark fabrics maintained their value when placed next to each other. I found a fabric that I thought was a medium value

Being able to audition the final fabric combination is my favorite aspect of the fast-forward method. Swap and rotate fabrics and units as needed to fine-tune the quilt. For me, a quilt may be great on paper but until I actually see how the fabrics interact, I don't make my final placement positions. When you look at your quilt, do you see a bit of sparkle? Do the light and dark fabrics help the pattern emerge? Use a reducing glass to view your quilt. Repeat what works and change what bothers you. Have fun experimenting and discovering how to use fabric to create beautiful quilts.

Fast-Forward Quilting with Interfacing

Gridded fusible interfacing will help you assemble a traditional quilt pattern quickly. Using fusible interfacing as a piecing foundation allows you to piece your blocks and join them in one step. Then, when you're ready to add borders, you can either fuse a pieced border onto interfacing, or you can sew uninterfaced border strips to the fused section of the quilt. If you choose the latter option, when you scrutinize the quilt you may notice a slight difference in thickness between the interfaced blocks and the uninterfaced borders. Quilting makes this difference very hard to see.

Fusible interfacings made of nonwoven polyester have long been used in garment sewing. To fast-forward your quilting, you can use the gridded variety as a piecing foundation. You simply lay out your cut shapes or pieced units on the gridded interfacing and fuse them in place. Fast-forward your quilt top to the finish line by folding and stitching the seams from top to bottom and side to side. You greatly reduce the amount of time spent on tedious chain piecing of individual pieces and units. Fusing pieces onto interfacing forgives wobbly rotary cutting and inaccurate unit piecing, and it absorbs slight fabric gaps and excesses. It also reduces the number of individual seams needed to construct a quilt top, increases accuracy, and anchors your designs in place before you sew the major seams. The fuse, fold, and stitch method is a wonderful way to join quilt blocks into a final setting ready for borders.

FUSING DESIGNS

Lay the interfacing on your work surface with the fusible side up. Double-check that you've posi-

tioned the interfacing correctly by running your fingers over the surface. You should feel the pebbly roughness of the adhesive dots on top. Once you're certain the interfacing is placed correctly, position the block units or plain pieces on the grid, right sides up. The fusible interfacing will be fused to the wrong side of the fabrics.

Align fabric edges with the interfacing grid. When placing units that include a diagonal seam, make that seam line your first consideration, not the straight edges of the unit. You want the diagonal seam angled precisely into opposite corners of the grid square.

Depending on your work surface, you may have difficulty seeing the grid lines well enough to align the units accurately. To make the grid easier to see, I sometimes slide the plastic direction sheet included with the interfacing, blank side up, underneath the interfacing. Because it's slippery, it's easy to remove and reposition. An alternative is to cover your work surface with white butcher paper. You might also consider covering your pressing surface with bright white cotton or flannel fabric to help you see the grid lines and protect your pressing surface from any fusible residue.

Adjust the height of your ironing board to match the height of your work surface, and then place the two next to each other. Gently pull a section of the interfacing panel onto the ironing board, and then line up pieces along the grid lines. Carefully positioning the units replaces the pinning you'd do with traditional piecing methods so be sure to do a good job on this step. For tips on positioning, see "Fast-Forward Units" on page 25. With the iron on a medium steam setting, press firmly for ten seconds. Repeat by lifting the iron and overlapping the previously fused section. Continue until the entire panel is fused.

You can peel off, reposition, and re-iron a section if necessary but do so only as a last resort. Removing a securely fused piece may distort or tear the bonding agent. Another option would be to cut out the unit. To do that, cut an interfacing patch larger than the piece you removed. Place it under the area removed. Fuse the patch and unit in place.

After fusing, allow the fabric to cool and then check the bond. Re-press as needed to ensure that there are no loose edges.

When working on quilts that are larger than your work surface, design and fuse in sections. An alternative is to lay out the quilt top on a design wall, and then transfer it in sections to the interfacing.

FOLDING AND STITCHING DESIGNS

Traditional piecing involves stitching units together and then joining those units to form blocks. The blocks are joined to form rows, and then the rows are joined. Fast-forward piecing allows you to skip the tedious individual unit-to-unit and block-to-block piecing. Instead, you can join all unit pairs along a row of the quilt top with one seam. The interfacing foundation lets you assemble the blocks and join them at the same time. You stitch vertical or horizontal seams, clip at seam intersections, and then stitch a second set of seams in the opposite direction.

1. Fold the interfacing panel between two rows, with right sides together.

2. Use a walking foot and stitch the first seam from top to bottom with a *scant* ¼"-wide seam allowance. Since you are stitching through four layers, which is different from normal piecing, the scant seam allowance allows for the bulk and ensures that the units will finish to the desired size. Stitch carefully so that the panel doesn't pull to one side at the beginning or end of a row; you don't want the long seam to curve.

3. Reversing your sewing direction, fold and stitch the next row from bottom to top. Alternate the sewing direction from row to row

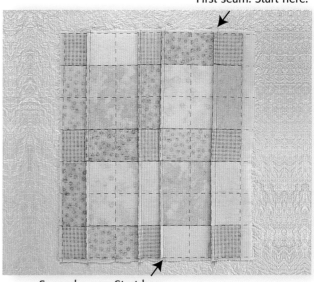

First seam. Start here.

Second seam. Start here.

Fold and stitch seams, alternating the stitching direction from row to row.

to balance any stretching of the seams due to the pull of the feed dogs. Alternating the sewing direction is especially helpful with diagonally set quilts because the stretch of the interfacing on the bias is aggravated if all rows are stitched in one direction. A walking foot may also help.

NOTE: *Interfacing panels tend to curl in on themselves as you sew. Be careful not to catch the edges of the panel as you stitch the rows of the quilt.*

4. At each row intersection, clip through the seam allowances to the stitching line. The ¼" snip will allow you to finger-press the seam allowances in opposite directions in the next step. Clip each intersection along each row. Do not cut the rows apart. Press seams from the front of the panel to counteract the panel's curling.

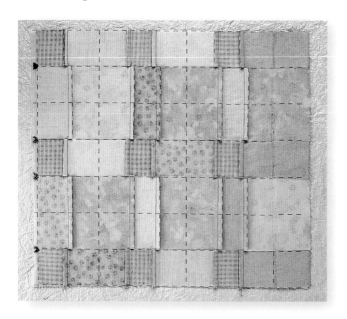

Clip rows to prepare for intersecting seams.

5. Join clipped panels with crosswise or lengthwise seams, if needed.

6. Fold the panel along the unstitched grid lines. Finger-press the clipped seam allowances in opposite directions to create snug intersections and prevent "speed bumps" (bulky intersections) from forming.

7. Stitch the remaining rows, using a scant ¼" seam allowance and alternating stitching directions from row to row. As you stitch, feel carefully with a fingertip to make sure that seam allowances are positioned correctly before they go under the needle.

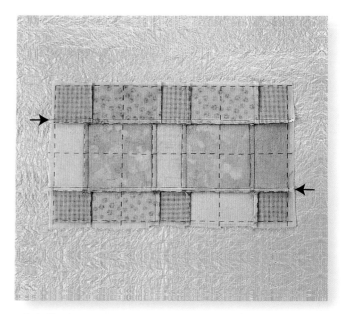

Stitch final seams.

8. Press the finished quilt top using lots of steam and a clean iron. Use a press cloth, if needed, when pressing the front to prevent transferring fusible-interfacing residue on the iron to the quilt top. Press well so that the seams lie flat.

➤➤ TIP: If you must join several panels to complete a larger quilt, stitch the initial fast-forward rows first. Then join the panels and sew the final fast-forward seams. You will avoid mismatched seams if you join the panels before you sew the final set of fast-forward seams. Refer to "Joining Interfacing Panels" on page 22 for more information.

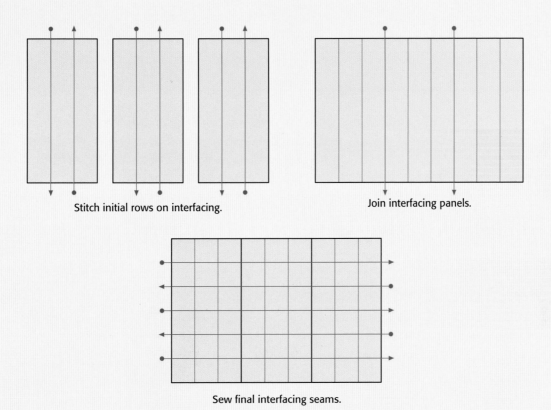

Stitch initial rows on interfacing.

Join interfacing panels.

Sew final interfacing seams.

Designing Fast-Forward Blocks and Quilts

There are three steps to designing successful fast-forward quilts. The first is to choose a block or blocks that can be constructed in units. The second is to plan the seams for the quilt top. And the third step is to cut and construct the units needed for the quilt top. One you complete these steps, you are ready to fast-forward your quilt using the fuse, fold, and stitch method.

The following section describes the selection process in detail, complete with examples to keep you on track. You'll learn to look at blocks differently and you'll notice how you can fast-forward your quilting.

CHOOSING THE BLOCKS

When choosing a block, first identify all seams that split the block from top to bottom and side to side. Many blocks are pieced with seams that can be sewn straight through from one side to the other. These horizontal and vertical seams are the planned fast-forward lines. Blocks with these intersecting seams can be made with the fuse, fold, and stitch technique.

Broken Dishes

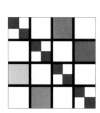

Carrie Nation

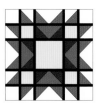

Memory

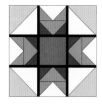

Corner Star

COMBINING BLOCKS

To use more than one type of block in a fast-forward quilt, simply combine blocks with similar fast-forward lines. Add or remove fast-forward lines as needed to allow you to combine blocks. Identifying the seams, or fast-forward lines, will indicate any units that need to be pieced prior to placing them on the fusible interfacing.

Broken Dishes

Carrie Nation with
4 Fast-Forward
Lines Removed

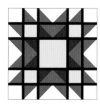

Memory

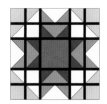

Corner Star with
4 Fast-Forward
Lines Added

PLANNING THE SEAMS FOR THE QUILT TOP

Once you've chosen your blocks, you are ready to plan your quilt-top seams. Will the quilt blocks have sashing and setting squares? Will the blocks be arranged in a straight set or in a diagonal set? Let's look at how these choices affect your fast-forward seams.

Sashing Strips

Sashing strips are an appealing way to frame blocks or tone down busy block combinations. Just keep in mind that you may need to divide the sashing into units to maintain the fast-forward seaming grid for your quilt. In "Indian Summer" on page 48, dividing the sashing into units allowed me to use several background fabrics and achieve a scrappy look. For a more uniform look, you could use the same fabric for all of the sashing pieces.

Sashing strips are a handy way to eliminate bulky intersections that result when several seams meet in the same place. To separate the Forget-Me-Not blocks shown below, you can add three sashing pieces of the desired width that match the length of the adjacent units.

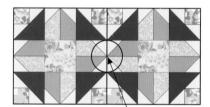

Eight seams meet at this point when Forget-Me-Not blocks are placed side by side.

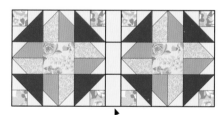

Placing a sashing strip between the blocks eliminates the bulky multi-point seam intersection.

Quilt-Top Settings

Blocks and sashing strips can be set either in straight rows or on point in a diagonal setting. The illustrations below show the two different setting options.

Straight Set

Diagonal Set

Straight-set quilts are easy to assemble, and each space is accounted for in the setting. There are no spaces to fill once all of the blocks are in place.

Diagonally set quilts, however, require the use of side and corner units to fill the spaces along the edges of the quilt. When planning your seams, extend the fast-forward lines needed to join the blocks to the edges of the quilt. The resulting setting pieces give you the opportunity to make a more interesting design. The resulting setting triangles can complete a secondary design formed by the blocks or act as a built-in border.

Add corner triangles and side setting units to square the quilt corners and complete the quilt. To create these units, first cut squares and then trim the excess, leaving enough fabric for a ¼" seam allowance. Determining how much fabric to trim is easy; just measure one edge of a side unit. Use that measurement as your cutting guide, but measure across the diagonal of the block. For instance, if your unit measures 4" x 4", you would measure and cut 4" from a corner, as shown.

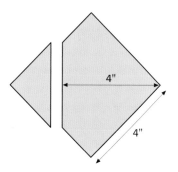

Save the trimmed corners. You'll place these pieces between the larger setting pieces to fill in gaps along the quilt edges.

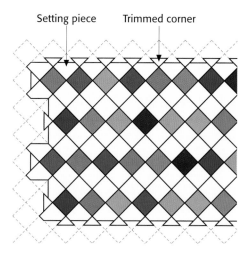

The setting units form a jagged line along the quilt edge. To straighten the edges after stitching, you can trim ¼" from the block points, or you can leave a wider seam allowance to float the block points against the background.

This is not the traditional way to create side and corner setting triangles, but it allows you to extend your fast-forward seam lines to the edges of the design.

This block features divided corner units. The version at left shows the initial layout, and the version at right shows the block after stitching. For an on-point design like this, you can trim the edges even with the large setting triangles, which leaves a portion of the small triangles visible in the finished block and also allows the dark block to float against the light background. Or, you can trim the edges ¼" from the dark points, in which case the small triangles disappear within the seam allowances.

EXPLORING DESIGN OPTIONS

Use the ideas in this book as a starting point, and then explore! Photocopy the blocks and quilt plans for your personal use, and then cut them apart and rearrange the pieces. Simply rotating block units can yield exciting possibilities. When I rotated and swapped the rectangle units used in "Water Lilies" on page 38, several different blocks emerged. Try similar experiments and have fun!

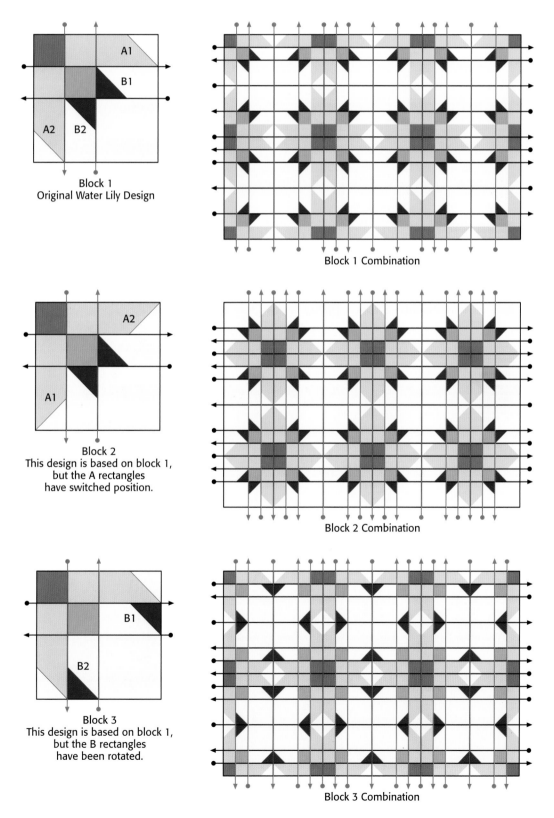

Block 1
Original Water Lily Design

Block 1 Combination

Block 2
This design is based on block 1,
but the A rectangles
have switched position.

Block 2 Combination

Block 3
This design is based on block 1,
but the B rectangles
have been rotated.

Block 3 Combination

Interfacing Basics: Straight and On-Point Grids

The first consideration in choosing a gridded fusible interfacing is which setting you will be using for your project—straight or on point. Note that for each project, you will find the quilt setting information in the section "Quilt Facts." At first you may think that selecting the interfacing is simple: straight-set interfacing for straight-set quilts, and on-point interfacing for diagonally set quilts. This works well until you can't find on-point interfacing.

If on-point interfacing is unavailable, simply purchase straight-set interfacing and arrange the units diagonally. To plan the interfacing layout, first sketch your on-point quilt design onto graph paper and cut it out. Then, on a different piece of graph paper that corresponds to the width of your straight-set interfacing, arrange the sketched quilt plan so that the seam lines align with the grid. Trim away sections of the quilt plan that overhang the grid and move them to an open space on the grid. The sections don't need to match up, as they will be joined later.

Stitching large panels of fused fabric can be cumbersome. Repeated handling can loosen the fusing bond, causing units to shift before you've stitched the seam that will secure them. Check the bond and re-fuse if needed. Large straight-set quilts can be divided into quarters and then stitched and joined traditionally if desired. Using straight-set interfacing for large, diagonally set quilts allows you to work in smaller panels and stitch all rows in one direction before you join the panels.

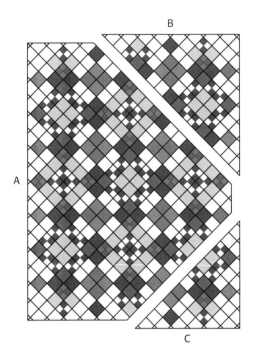

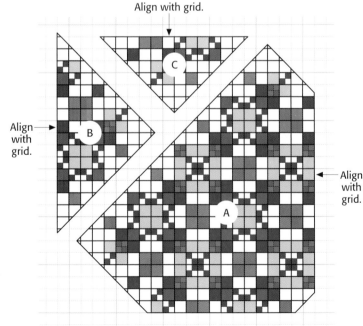

Converting Diagonal Settings for Straight-Set Interfacing

GRID SIZES

Students often wonder which interfacing to buy when the unit size or shape differs from the available printed grids. You can use any grid size; you just need to find a common measurement and use that to align the units. For example, when placing 3" units on a 2" grid, you must work in increments of 6 (2" x 3" = 6"). Two 3" block units will cover the same distance as three 2" squares across the grid, or 6".

As another example, a block of four 3" squares will cover the same area as a block of nine 2" squares. Begin by aligning the first square in one corner, and then work out from the corner. Two adjacent sides of each square will align with the grid lines.

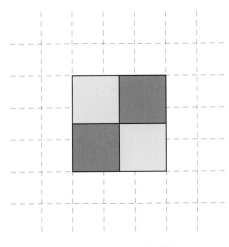

3" Squares on 2" Grid

You can also group units of different shapes and sizes. A 2½" square and a 4½"-long pieced rectangle combine to cover an area that's seven 1" grid squares long and 2½ squares wide. Two of these units placed side-by-side combine to form a 5" x 7" unit, which aligns perfectly on the 1" grid.

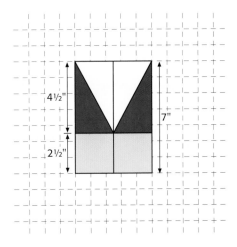

Two rectangles, one small square, and one large square will cover a 7" x 7" area of interfacing.

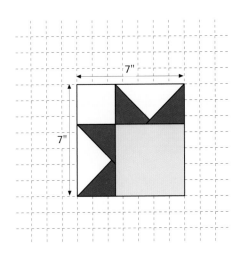

CALCULATING INTERFACING YARDAGE

After you decide to fast-forward your quilt, you need to determine how much interfacing is needed. Determine the area that the unfinished blocks, units, and sashing of your design will cover on interfacing and the number of blocks in your quilt. Remember to add ½" to finished measurements when calculating the size of the units before they are sewn. (See the charts on page 20).

CALCULATING YARDAGE FOR STRAIGHT-SET INTERFACING

Using 44"-wide interfacing, calculate the straight-set interfacing required for fast-forward piecing as follows.

Setting Width	Setting Length	Yardage Needed	Join
Up to 44" wide	Any length	Length ÷ 36"	—
Over 44" and up to 88" wide	No longer than 88"	(Width x 2) ÷ 36"	Crosswise
Over 44" and up to 88" wide	Longer than 88"	(Length x 2) ÷ 36"	Lengthwise
Over 88" wide	88" to 132"	(Width x 3) ÷ 36"	2 Crosswise

Straight-Set Interfacing

Straight-set interfacing is simple to use for fast-forward piecing. Note that on 44"-wide interfacing printed with a straight-set, 1"-grid, there are forty-four 1" squares from selvage to selvage, both on the diagonal and straight. This may seem obvious, but until I counted the squares I wondered.

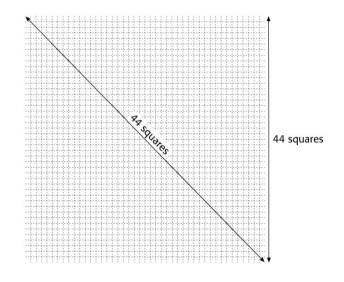

Diagonally Set Interfacing

While on-point interfacing is 44" wide, there may be some questions regarding the grid and the number of squares it includes due to the diagonal setting. On-point interfacing with a 1" grid has thirty-one 1" squares printed on point across the 44" width, selvage to selvage. There are twenty-five 1" squares printed on-point in each yard (36" in length) of interfacing. When calculating interfacing yardage for diagonally set quilts, allow an additional

CALCULATING YARDAGE FOR ON-POINT INTERFACING

Calculate the on-point interfacing required for fast-forward piecing as follows. Yardage requirements are based on 44"-wide fusible interfacing.

Setting Width	Setting Length	Yardage Needed	Join
Up to 31" wide	Any length	Length ÷ 25"	None
Over 31" and up to 62" wide	No longer than 62"	(Width x 2) ÷ 25"	Crosswise
Over 31" and up to 62" wide	Longer than 62"	(Length x 2) ÷ 25"	Lengthwise
Over 62" wide	62" to 93"	(Width x 3) ÷ 25"	2 Crosswise

1" on each side for the side triangles and corners used in the setting. Convert inches needed to yards by dividing inches needed by 25, since there are twenty-five 1" on-point squares per yard of interfacing.

As an example, let's calculate interfacing yardage for a diagonally set quilt that is four blocks wide and five blocks long. Each block is made up of nine units, each 3" x 3" finished. Each unfinished unit will cover a 3½" on-point square on the interfacing grid, and each unfinished block will cover a 10½" on-point square. To figure out how wide the interfacing needs to be, multiply the number of horizontal blocks by the unfinished size of the blocks (note that even though we're calculating an on-point setting, we're using the side-to-side block measurement rather than the corner-to-corner measurement). So, 4 blocks x 10½" = 42". To figure out how long the interfacing needs to be, multiply the number of vertical blocks by the size of the unfinished blocks. So, 5 blocks x 10½" = 52½".

We need to allow an additional 1" all around for the setting triangles and corners, which means we add 2" each to the length and width (42" + 2" = 44"; 52½" + 2" = 54½"), which gives us 44" x 54½". That's how much interfacing we need for the quilt.

In the Calculating Yardage for On-Point Interfacing chart, we first look to the Setting Width column. Our 44" width falls within the 31" to 62" range. Moving to the Setting Length column, we see that our 54½" length falls within the "no longer than 62"" category, so we move on to the Inches Needed column and find that we should multiply the width of the quilt by 2 (44" x 2" = 88"). The quilt requires an 88" length of on-point interfacing. To determine the required yardage, we refer to the Yardage Calculation column, which tells us to divide the inches needed by 25 (88" ÷ 25 = 3.52). Rounding up brings us to 3⅝ yards of on-point interfacing. The Join column indicates that we'll need to join two 44"-wide pieces of interfacing

crosswise to make a foundation large enough for the quilt.

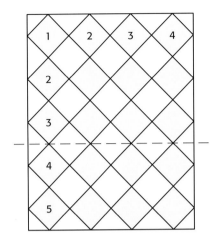

Unfinished block
as placed on interfacing

The same on-point quilt can be arranged on a straight-set interfacing grid. To convert a diagonal setting to a straight-set grid, begin by making a photocopy of the quilt plan. Cut the plan into sections that correspond to the width of the interfacing, allowing a 2" gap between quilt sections.

Again, each block in our example quilt covers a 10½" square of gridded interfacing. Since the interfacing is 44" wide, we can fit 4 blocks across it (4 blocks x 10½" = 42"). Dividing the quilt plan into 4-block widths results in the layout shown on the following page—3 sections that, taken together, total 4 blocks wide by 10 blocks long, with 2" gaps between the sections.

To figure out how much interfacing you need, multiply the number of vertical blocks by the side-to-side measurement of a block (10 blocks x 10½" = 105"). Then add the length of any gaps between sections (2 x 2" = 4" + 105" = 109"). On the interfacing layout, you'll see that two setting triangles overhang the straight-set block arrangement. To make sure you have a margin of foundation on which to fuse these pieces, just add 1" to the edges on which they'll be placed (42" + 2" = 44"). This brings us to final dimensions of 44" x 109". To determine the required yardage, refer to the Calculating Yardage for Straight-Set Interfacing chart on page 20. Since the layout is 44"-wide, we follow the first row of the chart and divide the length by 36 (109" ÷ 36 = 3.02), which rounds up to 3¼ yards of interfacing.

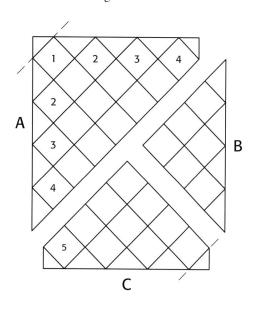

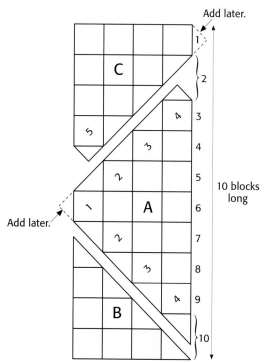

JOINING INTERFACING PANELS

When using printed interfacing, just cut the grid to the size you need. To determine interfacing yardage for any project, see "Calculating Interfacing Yardage" on page 19. If the interfacing isn't large enough, lay out and fuse your quilt in sections. Leave approximately 1" of grid for overlapping the panel seams. Since smaller panels are easier to work with, stitch all of the first set of rows except the joining seams. Align the panels, overlapping grids and butting edges of units. Fuse in place and then stitch. If you prefer not to fuse panels together, an alternative is to join them traditionally with a ¼" seam. After joining the panels, stitch the second set of fast-forward seams.

SQUARING PANELS

Before you add borders, check to see if the panel is square. A few diagonal tugs may remedy some distortions. For major distortions, you can block the quilt in sections by pinning it square and pressing the panel with a damp press cloth. Also try pinning the quilt top square on a carpet and then blocking it by spraying it with water and allowing it to dry. If you are unsure of the colorfastness of your quilt, test an area first before using any water.

If necessary, trim the edges square by aligning the center seams with the lines of a cutting mat. Then align your ruler with each edge and trim the excess. A line of stay stitching less than ¼" from the edge will keep seam allowances from flipping and edges from stretching.

If you had to trim away a lot to square the panel, vow to increase your accuracy on the next project. Quilting will hide or camouflage piecing imperfections. Enjoy the beauty you create and let your skills improve as you continue.

Basic Construction Information

Here are some quilting basics to assist you in constructing units for your fast-forward quilt.

ROTARY CUTTING BASIC MEASUREMENTS

Most quilt patterns are formed from a combination of the following shapes. When you know the basics of cutting, you can draft and adapt countless blocks and confidently calculate cutting directions.

Squares and rectangles are sub-cut from strips that are ½" wider than the finished width of the shape, which allows for a ¼" seam allowance all around.

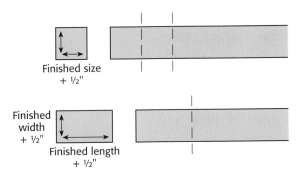

Finished size + ½"

Finished width + ½"

Finished length + ½"

Half-square triangles are cut from squares that are ⅞" wider than the finished measurement of the short side of the triangle. The cut triangles include ¼" for seams all around. In these triangles, the grain runs parallel to the short sides of the shape.

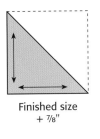

Finished size + ⅞"

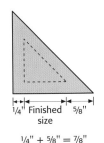

¼" Finished size ⅝"

¼" + ⅝" = ⅞"

Quarter-square triangles are cut from squares 1¼" wider than the finished measurement of the long side of the triangle. While quarter-square triangles have the same shape as a half-square triangle, the difference is that the grain runs parallel to the long side of the shape. When planning how to cut pieces for a quilt, your goal should be to have the grain run parallel to the outside edges of a block or unit.

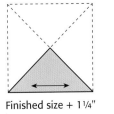

Finished size + 1¼"

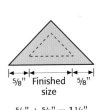

⅝" Finished size ⅝"

⅝" + ⅝" = 1¼"

Tall triangles that finish twice as high as they are wide are cut from rectangles. The cut rectangle is 1¼" wider than the long side of the finished triangle and ¾" wider than the short side of the finished triangle.

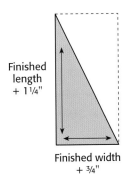

Finished length + 1¼"

Finished width + ¾"

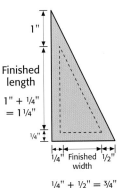

1"

Finished length

1" + ¼" = 1¼"

¼"

¼" Finished ½" width

¼" + ½" = ¾"

Many quilt patterns require that these triangles be placed with the diagonal seam facing in opposite directions. These are often called reverse units. To create a left and a right unit, cut four rectangles and then cut each set diagonally in opposite directions. You will combine one triangle cut from each set of rectangles to make a left and a right unit. The quilt "Hothouse Tulips" on page 59 uses the Six Tulips block and demonstrates the use of these triangles.

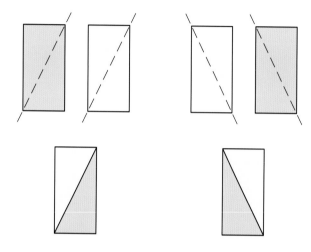

PIECING UNITS

Stitching with a consistent ¼" seam allowance is the most important rule in quilting. Some sewing machines have a special ¼" foot, which means you can use the edge of that presser foot as a guide against the raw edges of your patches to help maintain a ¼" seam allowance. Another option is to use the edge of your current presser foot and to adjust your needle position to the left or right so that your stitches are ¼" away from the needle. Yet another option is to create a seam guide by placing a piece of tape or moleskin ¼" away from the needle. You would use the edge of the tape as your sewing guide.

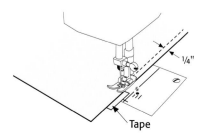

Tape

CHAIN PIECING

Chain piecing is an efficient system that saves time and thread. To use this technique, follow these steps:

1. With right sides together, place all the pieces that are to be joined in pairs with the side to be sewn to the right. Start sewing with the same edge on each pair and the same color on top to avoid confusion.

2. Feed each pair of fabrics into the machine one at a time without cutting the threads in between each one.

3. When all the pieces are sewn, take your chain to the ironing board. Press and clip the chain apart.

PRESSING

The traditional rule in quiltmaking is to press both seams to one side, generally toward the darker fabric. When joining two seamed units, plan ahead and press the seam allowances in opposite directions as shown. This reduces bulk and 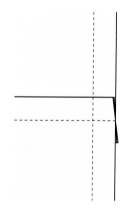 makes it easier to match corners and points. The seam allowances will butt against each other where two seams meet.

When pairs of triangles are sewn together, the stitching lines should cross each other on the back, creating an X. As you sew triangle units, sew with the triangle units on top, if possible, and aim to stitch directly through the X. This will maintain crisp points on the triangles.

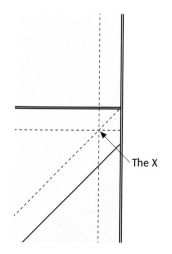

The X

Fast-Forward Units

The quilts in this book are designed from units commonly seen in quilting. The accuracy of quilts made with traditional methods depends on how accurately the fabric is cut and sewn using a ¼" seam allowance. While this sounds simple to master, it is a skill that requires practice and can frustrate beginners. Piecing with interfacing allows for some fudge factor. Small mistakes, less than ¼", can be lessened or corrected as the units are fused in place. Yes, even beginners can achieve an accurately pieced quilt even if their units are not so perfect.

For each unit described in the following sections, I've included my preferred method of construction. There are many ways to piece the different units and I encourage you to use the method that best suits your needs.

FOLDED-SQUARE TRIANGLE UNITS

Make a triangle corner by sewing a square to a rectangle or another square. Flip the square open and this becomes the triangle. Cut one square for the triangle corner the finished width of the triangle plus ½".

1. Fold the triangle square in half diagonally and lightly press a crease to mark the stitching line.

If you prefer, draw a diagonal line on the wrong side of the square.

Fold and crease.

2. With right sides together, place the square as indicated in the project directions.

3. Chain piece multiple units, sewing on the diagonal line. Trim the seam allowance to ¼". Press seams toward the triangles and clip apart units.

4. When possible, align the diagonal seam line of the unit with opposite corners of the interfacing grid lines and match neighboring units as well.

>> TIP: To make sewing folded-square triangles a little easier, put tape in front of the presser foot, perfectly aligning one edge of the tape with the needle. As you sew, follow the edge of the tape with the corner of the square. Using this technique, you won't have to fold or draw a diagonal line. Sewing larger squares simply requires a longer length of tape.

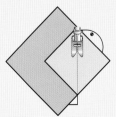

FOUR-PATCH UNITS

Four-patch units are finished square units divided into four quadrants. Cut strips for the patches the finished width of an individual small square plus ½". For example, a four-patch unit that finishes to 5" will have four small squares, each finishing 2½" x 2½". The strips would need to be cut 3" wide. The following steps explain how to make the units:

1. Cut strips the size given in the quilt directions. With right sides together, sew the strips together along their long edges. Press the seam toward the darker fabric.

2. Make two strip sets or cut a single strip set in half. Lay one strip set right side up and the other strip set right side down on top of it, butting the seams together. Cut the segment the width of the original strip and leave the pairs together because they are ready for sewing.

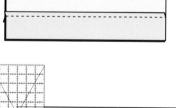

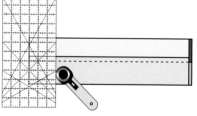

3. Chain piece the segment pairs, making sure the seams remain butted together. Clip the units apart and then press.

4. On the interfacing, align the four-patch seam lines with the midpoint of the interfacing grid lines covered by the unit and then match the seams of neighboring units.

> ▶▶ TIP: If you are drafting your own design, four-patch units that measure to whole numbers are easiest to work with on interfacing. For example, a unit that measures 3½" square in a finished quilt will cover 4" x 4" on interfacing.

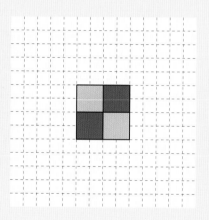

FAVORITE FOUR-PATCH UNIT SIZES

Finished Unit	Width of Cut Strip	Number of Units Per Strip Set (42"-wide strips)	Interfacing Covered
1½"	1¼"	16	2" x 2"
2½"	1¾"	11	3" x 3"
3½"	2¼"	8	4" x 4"
4½"	2¾"	7	5" x 5"

HALF-SQUARE-TRIANGLE UNITS

Half-square-triangle units are finished squares made by sewing two half-square triangles together. Cut a strip for each color of a unit the finished width plus ⅞". While there are many ways to make multiple half-square-triangle units, I prefer the following method because it is simple and wastes little fabric.

1. Cut strips the width given in the quilt directions. Pair strips by layering the two strip colors with right sides together. Fold the strip set in half crosswise. Align the edges and press the strip pair to reduce slipping while cutting and to remove any creases.

2. Cut squares from each layered pair of strips.

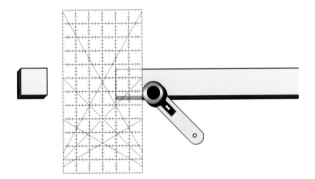

3. Use a long ruler to cut the layered squares once diagonally from corner to corner.

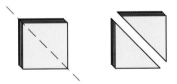

4. Chain piece the pairs, stitching the long edges together. Press seams toward the darker fabric. Clip apart units. Trim the points of the triangles even with the edge of each unit.

5. Align the diagonal seam line of the half-square-triangle units with the corners of the interfacing grid lines covered by the unit and then match the seams of neighboring units.

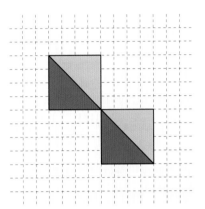

▶▶ TIP: If you are drafting your own design, half-square-triangle units that measure to whole numbers when placed on interfacing are easiest to work with. For example, a unit that measures 3½" square in a finished quilt will cover 4" x 4" on interfacing. The following chart gives quick cutting directions. Cut one square of each color to yield two half-square-triangle units.

FAVORITE HALF-SQUARE-TRIANGLE UNIT SIZES

Finished Unit	Size of Cut Square	Number of Units Per Strip Set (42"-wide strips)	Interfacing Covered
1½"	2⅜" x 2⅜"	34	2" x 2"
2½"	3⅜" x 3⅜"	24	3" x 3"
3½"	4⅜" x 4⅜"	18	4" x 4"
4½"	5⅜" x 5⅜"	14	5" x 5"

INSET SQUARES AND INSET TRIANGLES

Inset-square unit   Inset-triangle unit

Inset square units are half-square-triangle units with an inset square within one side of the unit. Inset triangle units are half-square-triangle units with an inset triangle, surrounded by three background triangles, within one side of the unit.

Sally Schneider simplified these units, sometimes called Shaded Four Patch units, in her book *Scrap Frenzy* (Martingale & Company, 2001). The following instructions are modified from Sally's method for template-free quick cutting.

1. For the inset piece, make two half-square-triangle units if you're making an inset triangle unit. Cut two plain squares the required size if you're making the inset square unit.

2. Cut two rectangles that are 1" longer than the squares. For example, if your half-square-triangle units or plain squares are 3" x 3", cut the rectangles 3" x 4". The square or half-square triangle should measure half the width of the finished inset-square unit.

3. Sew the rectangles to the half-square-triangle units or plain squares as shown. Press the seam toward the rectangles.

4. Sew the pairs of pieced units together. In the center of each unit, clip the seam allowance so that you can press the seams toward the rectangles.

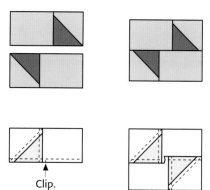

Clip.

5. Place each pieced unit right sides together on top of a same-size rectangle of another fabric. Align the 45° line on a ruler with the edge of the unit. Cut the units apart, leaving a ¼" seam allowance on each unit.

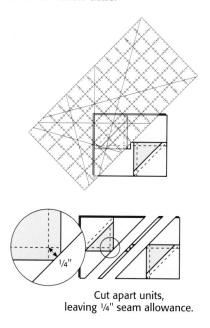

Cut apart units,
leaving ¼" seam allowance.

>> TIP: If you are drafting your own design, inset square or triangle units that measure to whole numbers when placed on interfacing are easiest to work with. For example, a unit that measures 3½" square on a finished quilt will cover 4" x 4" on interfacing with the diagonal seam aligned corner to corner.

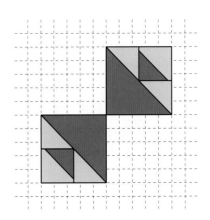

6. Chain piece the long side of the pairs together, aiming your stitching to intersect the X on the inset corner piece. Press the seams toward the large, plain triangle.

7. Align the diagonal seam line of the triangle units with the corners of the interfacing grid lines covered by the unit and match the seams of neighboring units.

FAVORITE INSET-SQUARE AND INSET-TRIANGLE UNIT SIZES

Finished Unit	Size of Plain Square of Half-Square-Triangle Unit	Cut Size of 1st Rectangle	Cut Size of 2nd Rectangle	Interfacing Covered
3½" x 3½"	1¾" x 1¾"	2¼" x 3¼"	4" x 5"	4" x 4"
4½" x 4½"	2¼" x 2¼"	2¾" x 3¾"	5" x 6"	5" x 5"
5½" x 5½"	2¾" x 2¾"	3¼" x 4¼"	6" x 7"	6" x 6"

FLYING-GEESE UNITS

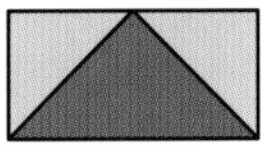

Flying-geese units finish twice as long as wide. They use a half-square triangle on each end with a quarter-square triangle in the center. You can create the shape by using folded-square triangles on page 25. I learned another easy technique from quilting teacher Billie Lauder. Cut one large square the long finished width plus 1¼" and four small squares the short finished height plus ⅞". This method yields four flying-geese units from each set of squares.

1. Fold all small squares diagonally and press a crease or draw a diagonal line on the wrong side from corner to corner. Trim ⅜" off a corner of two small squares. Unfold the squares.

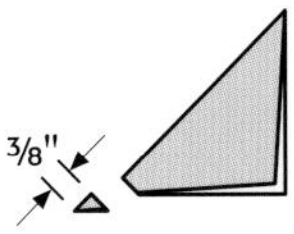

2. With right sides together, place two trimmed small squares on the large square, with both diagonal lines running continuously from corner to corner. Trimmed corners will meet in the center. Sew ¼" away on both sides of the crease or drawn diagonal line.

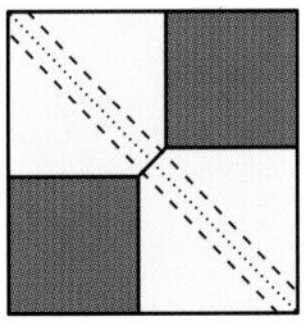

3. Cut on the center crease or line. Press seam allowances toward the small triangles. You now have two heart-shaped units.

4. With right sides together, place one of the remaining small squares on the large triangle with the crease or diagonal line placed into the corner. Sew ¼" away on both sides of the crease or line. Repeat for the second unit.

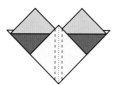

5. Cut on the center crease or line. Press seam allowances toward the small triangles. Trim the seam allowance points. You now have four flying-geese units.

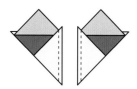

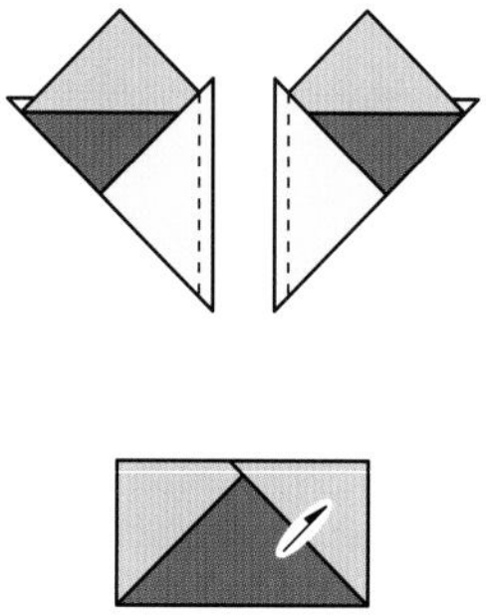

Make 4.

6. Align the seam lines of the unit with the interfacing grid lines and the seam lines of any neighboring units.

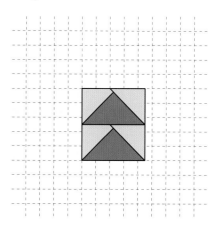

➤➤ Some flying-geese sizes work better on grids than others. If you are drafting your own design, the flying-geese units in the chart below are easiest to corral when placed on interfacing. The following chart gives quick cutting instructions to yield four flying-geese units from each large square.

FAVORITE FLYING-GEESE UNIT SIZES

Finished Unit	4 Small Squares	1 Large Square	Interfacing Covered
1½" x 3"	2⅜"	4¼"	2" x 3½"
2" x 4"	2⅞"	5¼"	2½" x 4½"
2½" x 5"	3⅜"	6¼"	3" x 5½"
3" x 6"	3⅞"	7¼"	3½" x 6½"

TALL TRIANGLES

Tall triangle units finish twice as long as wide, with the rectangle divided in half diagonally. The diagonal seam can cross the unit from the left or from the right. For the units, cut one rectangle of each color the finished length plus 1¼", and the finished width plus ¾". This method yields equal numbers of left and right units.

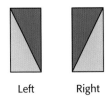

Left   Right

1. Cut strips the size given in the quilt directions. Pair strips by layering the two strip colors with right sides together. Fold the strip set in half crosswise. Align the edges and press the strip pair to reduce slipping and to remove all creases.

2. Cut rectangles from each layered pair of strips.

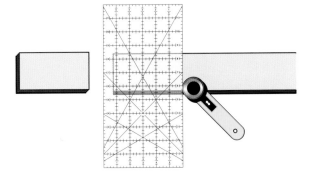

3. Use a long ruler to cut the layered rectangles once diagonally from corner to corner.

4. Trim the tall points. Photocopy or trace the tall triangle trimming template pattern shown below, noting the grain lines and the trimming line. The template is actual size and does not need to be enlarged. Tape the template to a see-through ruler, with the trimming line against the edge of the ruler and the triangle tip in an easily seen portion of the ruler. Align the template over the tall tip of the triangle, with the grain line along the straight edge, not the slant edge, and trim off.

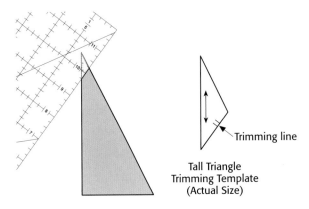

← Trimming line

Tall Triangle
Trimming Template
(Actual Size)

5. Pair two tall triangles with right sides together and tall points going in opposite directions. Line up the ends. Chain piece the pairs, stitching along the long edges. Press seams toward the dark fabric and clip apart the units. Trim the seam-allowance points.

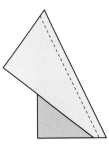

6. Align the edges of the tall triangle units on gridded interfacing, with the diagonal seam line placed ⅛" in from the corner of the grid on the short side of the rectangle, and then match the seams of neighboring units.

FAVORITE TALL TRIANGLE UNIT SIZES

Finished Unit	Size of Cut Rectangle	Interfacing Covered
1½" x 3"	2¼" x 4¼"	2" x 3½"
2" x 4"	2¾" x 5¼"	2½" x 4½"
2½" x 5"	3¼" x 6¼"	3" x 5½"
3" x 6"	3¾" x 7¼"	3½" x 6½"

➤➤ TIP: To check that diagonal seam was pieced accurately, align the view-finder end of a Ruby Beholder with the edges of the tall triangle unit as shown. The ¼"-wide border of the view-finder opening will cover the seam allowances. If the tall triangle was pieced accurately, the diagonal seam will intersect the corner of the opening.

Check diagonal seam intersection.

➤➤ TIP: If you are drafting your own design, tall triangle units that are whole numbers when placed on interfacing are easiest to corral. For example, two units that measure 2" x 4" on a finished quilt will cover 5" x 4½" on interfacing before sewing. The chart above gives quick cutting directions. Cut one rectangle of each color to yield two tall triangle units.

Fossil Fantasy

By Dina Pappas, 33½" x 42½". Quilted by Marguerita McManus. I used all 150 fabrics of the Benartex Fossil Fern collection and a gray fabric to divide and frame the color fabrics. A picture of a sunset, with its changing shades, gave me a starting point to work from. Marguerita used a circular quilting pattern with 15 thread colors to tie it all together. This is a great pattern with which to create an I Spy quilt with children. The quilt shown here is the wall-hanging size.

QUILT FACTS

	Wall Hanging	Crib	Double
Finished size	33½" x 42½"	39" x 49"	74" x 81"
Block set	9 x 12 straight	6 x 8 straight	9 x 10 straight
Finished block size	2½" x 2½"	3½" x 3½"	5½" x 5½"
Unfinished block size on interfacing	3" x 3"	4" x 4"	6" x 6"
Finished sashing size	½" x 2½"	1½" x 3½"	1½" x 5½"
Sashing size on interfacing	1" x 3"	2" x 4"	2" x 6"

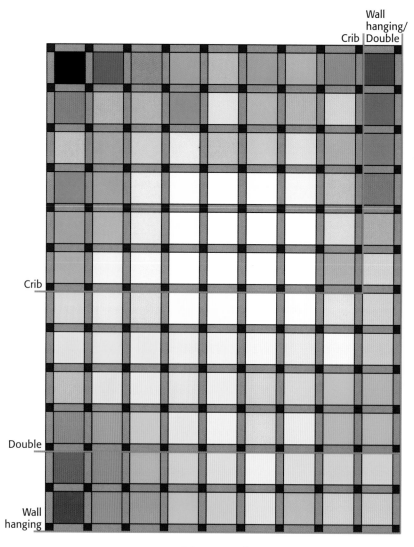

Master Design

MATERIALS

Yardage is based on 42"-wide fabric.

	Wall Hanging	Crib	Double
Sashing and border background	1¼ yards	¾ yard	2⅛ yards
Colored squares			
(total yardage required of assorted prints)	1⅛ yards	¾ yard	2⅞ yards
Posts and binding	½ yard	¾ yard	1⅛ yards
Unpieced border	–	¾ yard	1⅜ yards
Backing	1⅜ yards	2½ yards*	5 yards**
Batting	38" x 47"	43" x 53"	78" x 85"
Straight-set fusible interfacing for quilt center only	1⅝ yards†	1⅝ yards	5 yards
On-point fusible interfacing for border only	2 yards	–	–

* Two widths pieced horizontally
** Two widths pieced vertically
† If using straight-set interfacing for both blocks and border, you will need 3¼ yards.

CUTTING FOR WALL-HANGING SIZE

All strips are cut across the width of the fabric.

Fabric	Number of 42"-Long Strips	Strip Width	Piece Length	Pieces
Colored squares	12	3"	3"	150
Sashing and border				
background	19	1"	3"	237
	6	3"	3"	71
Posts	4	1"	1"	130
Binding	5	2½"	–	–
Straight-set interfacing	1	37"	49"	–

CUTTING FOR CRIB SIZE

All strips are cut across the width of the fabric.

Fabric	Number of 42"-Long Strips	Strip Width	Piece Length	Pieces
Colored squares	5	4"	4"	48
Sashing	11	2"	4"	110
Posts	4	2"	2"	63
Border	5	4"	–	–
Binding	5	2½"	–	–
Straight-set interfacing	1	38"	50"	–

CUTTING FOR DOUBLE SIZE

All strips are cut across the width of the fabric.

Fabric	Number of 42"-Long Strips	Strip Width	Piece Length	Pieces
Colored squares	15	6"	6"	90
Sashing	34	2"	6"	199
Posts	6	2"	2"	110
Border	8	5"	—	—
Binding	9	2½"	—	—
Straight-set interfacing	2	38"	82"	—

FAST-FORWARD PIECING ❯❯❯

1. Place the interfacing grid on your work surface, fusible side up. Following the master design for your quilt size on page 34, arrange the sashing, posts, and blocks on interfacing. For the wall-hanging size only: To coordinate the wall-hanging center and borders, the border squares need to be arranged now and then set aside. The goal is to form a pleasing arrangement using 108 of the squares (set 9 x 12) in the center and 42 squares (9 for the top and bottom, 12 for each side) for the border. Once you've come up with a pleasing arrangement, make notes regarding placement of the border pieces or take a snapshot for reference, and then set aside the border squares.

2. Evaluate your design. Make adjustments by replacing or rotating squares as needed. Set aside the wall-hanging border squares, maintaining the arranged order.

3. Straighten the pieces on the grid. Fuse the pieces in place.

4. Fold and stitch the interfacing panel. Finger-press the seam allowances toward the sashing.

PIECED BORDER FOR WALL-HANGING SIZE

1. Trim eleven border squares for setting points.

2. Place the on-point interfacing grid on your work surface, fusible side up. Following the border plan below, arrange the colored border squares and background squares on the interfacing for each side of the quilt.

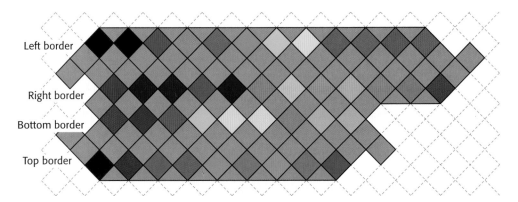

Border Plan
Note: Wall-hanging size *only*.

3. Straighten the pieces on the grid. Fuse the squares in place.

4. Fold and stitch the interfacing pane, using a generous ⅜" seam allowance—in order for the pieced border strips to best fit the quilt, it is necessary to adjust the seam allowance.

5. Cut apart the border segments as shown, leaving a ¼" seam allowance along the bias edge of the triangles to stitch next to quilt. Cut borders 3¼" wide, placing the ¼" line of your ruler directly over the intersections of the colored squares. Pin to fit and stitch the borders to the wall hanging, mitering the corners. For the best fit, match and pin the triangles at both ends of the border to the end of the quilt. Also, match the middle of the border to the middle of the quilt and pin evenly along the edge to distribute the slight fullness evenly. Sew with the fuller edge on the bottom of the machine next to the feed dogs.

QUILT FINISHING

1. For crib and double sizes, refer to "Straight-Cut Borders" on page 104 to measure and sew the border strips to the quilt top.

2. Layer the backing, batting, and quilt top; baste the layers together. Quilt as desired. Bind the quilt edges. See "Finishing Techniques," starting on page 104, for specific details on quilting and binding.

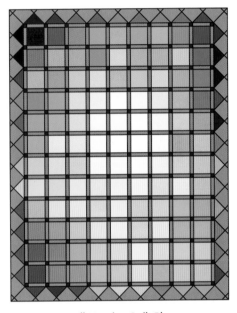

Wall-Hanging Quilt Plan

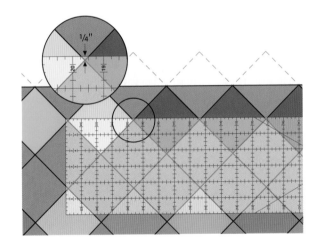

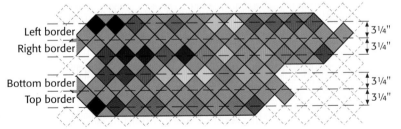

Left border
Right border
Bottom border
Top border

3¼"
3¼"
3¼"
3¼"

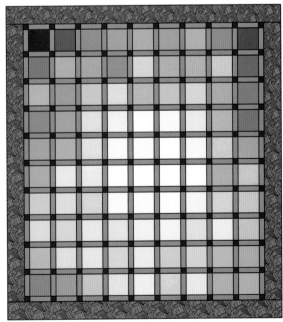

Double Quilt Plan

Water Lilies

By Dina Pappas and Mary E. LaTour, 48½" x 48½". Quilted by Judy Bolechala. While the colors are simple blues and greens, the variety of fabrics is what adds a real punch. The quilt shown here is the wall-hanging size.

QUILT FACTS

	Wall Hanging	Twin	Queen
Finished size	48½" x 48½"	59½" x 81½"	81½" x 81½"
Block set	6 x 6 straight	8 x 12 straight	12 x 12 straight
Blocks	36	96	144
Finished block size	5½" x 5½"	5½" x 5½"	5½" x 5½"
Unfinished block size on interfacing	7" x 7"	7" x 7"	7" x 7"

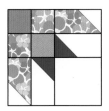

Water Lily Block

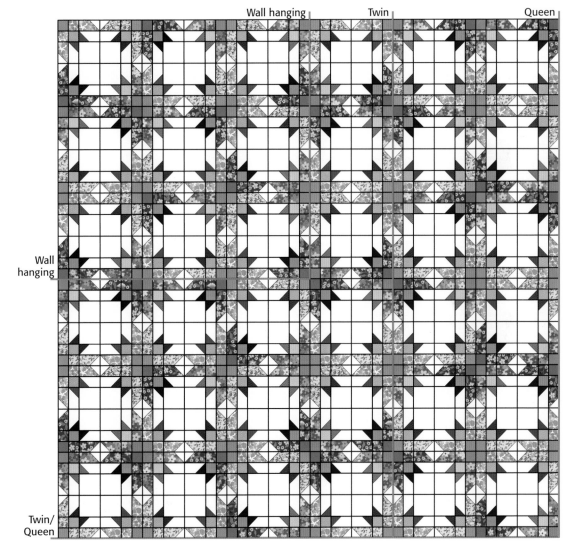

Master Design

NOTE: *Block and setting options for this quilt are shown on page 17.*

MATERIALS

Yardage is based on 42"-wide fabric.

	Wall Hanging	Twin	Queen
Background	1 yard	2⅜ yards	3½ yards
Florals for blocks	¾ yard	1⅝ yards	2⅜ yards
Middle border	¾ yard	1 yard	1⅜ yards
Outer border	⅝ yard	¾ yard	¾ yard
Darks for blocks	⅜ yard	¾ yard	1 yard
Inner border	⅜ yard	½ yard	⅝ yard
Lights for blocks	¼ yard	⅜ yard	⅝ yard
Mediums for blocks	¼ yard	⅜ yard	⅝ yard
Backing	3⅜ yards*	5¼ yards**	7¾ yards†
Binding	⅝ yard	¾ yard	¾ yard
Batting	53" x 53"	64" x 86"	86" x 86"
Straight-set fusible interfacing	1⅜ yards	3⅜ yards	4¾ yards

Two widths pieced horizontally or vertically
**Two widths pieced vertically*
† *Three widths pieced horizontally or vertically*

CUTTING FOR WALL-HANGING SIZE

All strips are cut across the width of the fabric.

Fabric	Number of 42"-Long Strips	Strip Width	Piece Length	Pieces
Background	4	2"	2"	72
	6	2"	3"	72
	3	3"	3"	36
Florals	4	2"	2"	72
	6	2"	3"	72
Darks	4	2"	2"	72
Lights	2	2"	2"	36
Mediums	2	2"	2"	36
Inner border	4	2"	—	—
Middle border	5	4½"	—	—
Outer border	6	2½"	—	—
Binding	6	2½"	—	—
Interfacing	1	42"	42"	—

CUTTING FOR TWIN SIZE

All strips are cut across the width of the fabric.

Fabric	Number of 42"-Long Strips	Strip Width	Piece Length	Pieces
Background	10	2"	2"	192
	15	2"	3"	192
	8	3"	3"	96
Florals	10	2"	2"	192
	15	2"	3"	192
Darks	10	2"	2"	192
Lights	5	2"	2"	96
Mediums	5	2"	2"	96
Inner border	7	2"	—	—
Middle border	7	4½"	—	—
Outer border	8	2½"	—	—
Binding	8	2½"	—	—
Interfacing	2	44"	56"	—

CUTTING FOR QUEEN SIZE

All strips are cut across the width of the fabric.

Fabric	Number of 42"-Long Strips	Strip Width	Piece Length	Pieces
Background	15	2"	2"	288
	23	2"	3"	288
	12	3"	3"	144
Florals	15	2"	2"	288
	23	2"	3"	288
Darks	15	2"	2"	288
Lights	8	2"	2"	144
Mediums	8	2"	2"	144
Inner border	8	2"	—	—
Middle border	9	4½"	—	—
Outer border	9	2½"	—	—
Binding	9	2½"	—	—
Interfacing	2	44"	84"	—

UNIT PIECING

1. Use the folded-square triangle technique to sew a 2" background square on top of each 2" x 3" floral rectangle. Sew half of the units and reverse remaining units as shown.

Make 1 per block.

Make 1 per block.

2. Use the folded-square triangle technique to sew a 2" dark square on top of each 2" x 3" background rectangle. On half of the units sew the square to the right-hand side and on the other half sew the square to the left-hand side, stitching as shown.

Make 1 per block.

Make 1 per block.

FAST-FORWARD PIECING ▶▶▶

1. Place the interfacing grid on your work surface, fusible side up. Following the master design for your quilt size on page 39, begin by placing folded-square units on the interfacing. Align diagonal seam lines with the corners of the grid.

2. Fill in the remaining grid with squares as indicated on the quilt plan.

3. Evaluate your design. Make any adjustments by replacing or rotating squares as needed.

4. Straighten the pieces on the grid. Fuse the pieces in place.

5. Fold and stitch the interfacing panel(s).

QUILT FINISHING

1. Refer to "Mitered Borders" on page 105 to measure and sew the border strips to the quilt top.

2. Layer the backing, batting, and quilt top; baste the layers together. Quilt as desired. Bind the quilt edges. See "Finishing Techniques," starting on page 104, for specific details on quilting and binding.

Twin Quilt Plan

≈ Argyle Stinger ≈

By Dina Pappas, 37" x 45½". The Stinger block evolved from the Carrie Nation block. After I changed colors and rotated units, the final block reminded me of a mosquito. This quilt shows that you can create an interesting overall design with just one block! The quilt shown here is the wall-hanging size.

QUILT FACTS

	Wall Hanging	Twin	Queen
Finished size	37" x 45½"	62⅞" x 77"	91⅛" x 105⅜"
Block set	3 x 4 diagonal	3 x 4 diagonal	5 x 6 diagonal
Total blocks	18 + 10 side units	18 + 10 side units	50 + 18 side units
Finished block size	6" x 6"	10" x 10"	10" x 10"
Unfinished block size on interfacing	8" x 8"	12" x 12"	12" x 12"

Argyle Stinger Block

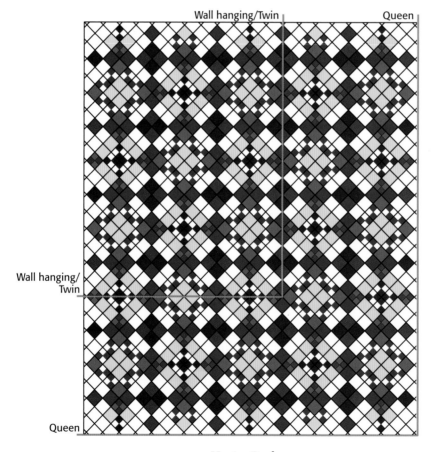

Master Design

MATERIALS

Yardage is based on 42"-wide fabric.

	Wall Hanging	Twin	Queen
Background	⅞ yard	1⅝ yards	3⅜ yards
Outer border	⅝ yard	2 yards	2⅞ yards
Blue for blocks	⅜ yard	¾ yard	1½ yards
Yellow for blocks	⅜ yard	⅝ yard	1¼ yards
Purple for blocks	⅜ yard	⅜ yard	⅞ yard
Inner border	⅜ yard	⅝ yard	⅞ yard
Light green for blocks	¼ yard	⅜ yard	⅞ yard
Dark green for blocks	¼ yard	⅜ yard	⅞ yard
Backing	1⅝ yards	5 yards*	8½ yards**
Binding	½ yard	¾ yard	1 yard
Batting	41" x 50"	67" x 81"	96" x 110"
On-point fusible interfacing	1⅝ yards	3¼ yards	6¼ yards
OR			
Straight-set fusible interfacing	1½ yards	3 yards	7½ yards

* Two widths pieced vertically
** Three widths pieced horizontally

CUTTING FOR WALL-HANGING SIZE

All strips are cut across the width of the fabric.

Fabric	Number of 42"-Long Strips	Strip Width	Piece Length	Pieces
Background	5	1¼"	—	—
	9	2"	2"	168
Dark green	2	1¼"	—	—
	1	2"	2"	20
Light green	2	1¼"	—	—
	1	2"	2"	20
Purple	2	1¼"	—	—
	2	2"	2"	22
Blue	3	1¼"	—	—
	2	2"	2"	40
Yellow	4	2"	2"	62
Inner border	4	2"	—	—
Outer border	4	4½"	—	—
Binding	5	2½"	—	—
On-point interfacing	1	26 squares	38 squares	—

CUTTING FOR TWIN SIZE

All strips are cut across the width of the fabric.

Fabric	Number of 42"-Long Strips	Strip Width	Piece Length	Pieces
Background	6	1¾"	—	—
	13	3"	3"	168
Dark green	2	1¾"	—	—
	2	3"	3"	20
Light green	2	1¾"	—	—
	2	3"	3"	20
Purple	2	1¾"	—	—
	2	3"	3"	22
Blue	4	3"	3"	40
	4	1¾"	—	—
Yellow	5	3"	3"	62
Inner border	6	3"	—	—
Outer border	8	8"	—	—
Binding	8	2½"	—	—
On-point interfacing	2	26 squares	39 squares	—

CUTTING FOR QUEEN SIZE

All strips are cut across the width of the fabric.

Fabric	Number of 42"-Long Strips	Strip Width	Piece Length	Pieces
Background	16	1¾"	—	—
	27	3"	3"	352
Dark green	5	1¾"	—	—
	5	3"	3"	54
Light green	5	3"	3"	54
	5	1¾"	—	—
Purple	5	1¾"	—	—
	5	3"	3"	56
Blue	11	1¾"	—	—
	9	3"	3"	108
Yellow	13	3"	3"	164
Inner border	9	3"	—	—
Outer border	11	8"	—	—
Binding	11	2½"	—	—
On-point interfacing	3	27 squares	63 squares	—

UNIT PIECING

1. Sew background strips to the dark green strips. Press seams toward the dark green. Layer strips as shown and crosscut each pair of strip sets the same width as the original strips.

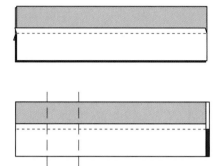

2. Chain-piece pairs from step 1 into four-patch units, making sure the seams butt together. Press seams and clip apart units.

3. Repeat steps 1 and 2 for remaining background strips and blue strips. Repeat steps 1 and 2 for the light green and the purple strips. Referring to the column for your quilt size, make the number of four-patch units listed in the chart below.

FAST-FORWARD PIECING ⟩⟩⟩

1. Place the interfacing grid on your work surface, fusible side up. Following the master design for your quilt size on page 44, place four-patch units on the interfacing. Align the unit seam lines with the grid lines.

2. Fill in the remaining grid with squares as indicated on the quilt plan.

3. Evaluate your design. Make any adjustments by replacing or rotating squares as needed.

4. Referring to "Quilt-Top Settings" on page 15, trim edge background squares into setting triangle units and setting points. Place setting triangle units and setting points on grid. Trim the edges as desired.

5. Straighten the pieces on the grid. Fuse the pieces in place.

6. Fold and stitch the interfacing panel(s).

QUILT FINISHING

1. Refer to "Mitered Borders" on page 105 to measure and sew the border strips to the quilt top.

2. Layer the backing, batting, and quilt top; baste the layers together. Quilt as desired. Bind the quilt edges. See "Finishing Techniques," starting on page 104, for specific details on quilting and binding.

Wall-Hanging/Twin Quilt Plan

NUMBER OF FOUR-PATCH UNITS

Strip Sets	Wall Hanging	Twin	Queen
Background and dark green	20 units	20 units	54 units
Background and blue	44 units	44 units	112 units
Light green and purple	20 units	20 units	54 units

Indian Summer

By Dina Pappas, 68" x 68". Green squares alter the traditional fabric placement for this design and create nice diagonal lines that unify the blocks. Without the sashing, the quilt would have a very different look. The quilt shown here is the lap size.

QUILT FACTS

	Lap	Twin	Queen
Finished size	68" x 68"	68" x 93"	93" x 93"
Block set	4 x 4 straight	4 x 6 straight	6 x 6 straight
Total blocks	16	24	36
Finished block size	10" x 10"	10" x 10"	10" x 10"
Unfinished block size on interfacing	11½" x 11½"	11½" x 11½"	11½" x 11½"
Finished sashing width	2½"	2½"	2½"
Sashing width on interfacing	3"	3"	3"

Indian Summer Block

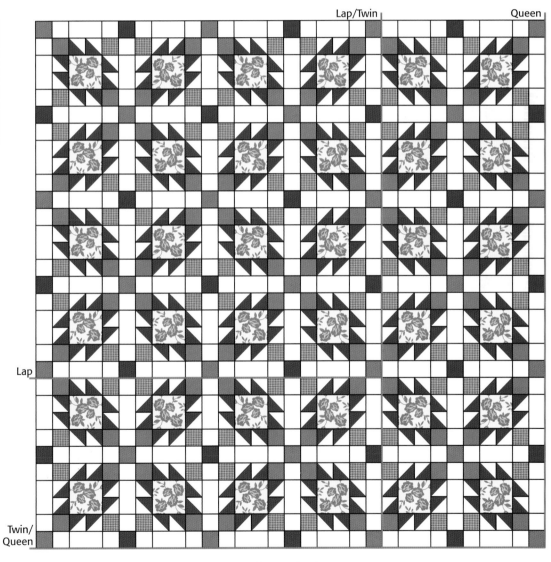

Master Design

MATERIALS

Yardage is based on 42"-wide fabric.

	Wall Hanging	Twin	Queen
Floral for blocks and border	2¼ yards	2⅝ yards	3 yards
Background	1⅞ yards	2⅝ yards	3¾ yards
Red for blocks and border	1⅛ yards	1⅝ yards	2¼ yards
Green for blocks and binding	1¼ yards	1⅜ yards	1½ yards
Light red for blocks	⅜ yard	½ yard	⅝ yard
Backing	4½ yards*	6 yards**	8½ yards†
Batting	72" x 72"	72" x 97"	97" x 97"
Straight-set fusible interfacing	3¾ yards	5½ yards	7¾ yards

* Two widths pieced horizontally or vertically
** Two widths pieced vertically
† Three widths pieced horizontally or vertically

CUTTING FOR LAP SIZE

All strips are cut across the width of the fabric.

Fabric	Number of 42"-Long Strips	Strip Width	Piece Length	Pieces
Background	6	3⅜"	—	—
	7	3"	3"	80
	6	3"	5½"	40
Red	6	3⅜"	—	—
	1	3"	3"	12
	6	2"	—	—
Green	4	3"	3"	45
Light red	3	3"	3"	32
Floral	3	5½"	5½"	16
	8	6½"	—	—
Binding	8	2½"	—	—
Interfacing	2	—	61"	—

CUTTING FOR TWIN SIZE

All strips are cut across the width of the fabric.

Fabric	Number of 42"-Long Strips	Strip Width	Piece Length	Pieces
Background	9	3⅜"	—	—
	9	3"	3"	116
	9	3"	5½"	58
Red	9	3⅜"	—	—
	2	3"	3"	17
	8	2"	—	—
Green	6	3"	3"	66
Light red	4	3"	3"	48
Floral	4	5½"	5½"	24
	9	6½"	—	—
Binding	9	2½"	—	—
Interfacing	2	—	90"	—

CUTTING FOR QUEEN SIZE

All strips are cut across the width of the fabric.

Fabric	Number of 42"-Long Strips	Strip Width	Piece Length	Pieces
Background	14	3⅜"	—	—
	13	3"	3"	168
	12	3"	5½"	84
Red	14	3⅜"	—	—
	2	3"	3"	24
	9	2"	—	—
Green	8	3"	3"	97
Light red	6	3"	3"	72
Floral	6	5½"	5½"	36
	10	6½"	—	—
Binding	10	2½"	—	—
Interfacing	3	—	90"	—

UNIT PIECING

1. With right sides together, layer pairs of 3⅜"-wide background strips and red strips. Cut strip pairs into 3⅜" squares, keeping them in sets. Cut the square sets diagonally from corner to corner.

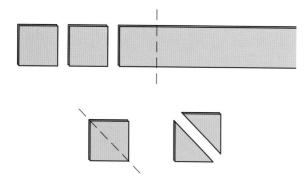

2. Chain piece the pairs along the long edge. Press seams toward the red triangles and clip triangle sets apart. Join two half-square triangles to form square units.

Make 2 per block. Make 2 per block.

FAST-FORWARD PIECING ⟩⟩⟩

1. Place the interfacing grid on your work surface, fusible side up. Following the master design for your quilt size on page 49, place half-square-triangle units on the interfacing. Align the diagonal seam lines with the corners of the grid.

2. Fill in the remaining grid with squares as indicated on the quilt plan.

3. Evaluate your design. Make any adjustments by replacing or rotating squares as needed.

4. Straighten the pieces on the grid. Fuse the pieces in place.

5. Fold and stitch the interfacing panel(s).

QUILT FINISHING

1. Refer to "Mitered Borders" on page 105 to measure and sew the border strips to the quilt top.

2. Layer the backing, batting, and quilt top; baste the layers together. Quilt as desired. Bind the quilt edges. See "Finishing Techniques," starting on page 104, for specific details on quilting and binding.

Twin Quilt Plan

Woven Nations

By Dina Pappas, 49½" x 56½". Two colors of Carrie Nation blocks weave through the Broken Dishes blocks. This quilt was inspired by Donna Lynn Thomas's book *Scrappy Duos.* After making a jacket using these blocks, I realized that I could have used the fast-forward method and 75% fewer seams. I wish I'd thought of it sooner. The quilt shown here is the lap size.

QUILT FACTS

	Lap	Twin	Queen
Finished size	49½" x 63½"	68½" x 88"	82¼" x 107¾"
Block set	5 x 7 diagonal	5 x 7 diagonal	5 x 7 diagonal
Total blocks	59 + 20 side units	59 + 20 side units	59 + 20 side units
Finished block size	5" x 5"	7" x 7"	9" x 9"
Unfinished block size on interfacing	6" x 6"	8" x 8"	10" x 10"

Broken Dishes Block

Carrie Nation Block

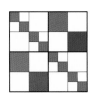

Carrie Nation Block

Master Design

MATERIALS

Yardage is based on 42"-wide fabric.

	Lap	Twin	Queen
Background	1⅜ yards	2 yards	3 yards
Outer border	1¼ yards	2 yards	2¼ yards
Mediums for blocks	1⅛ yards	1½ yards	2⅜ yards
Darks for blocks	¾ yard	1⅛ yards	1¾ yards
Inner border	½ yard	¾ yard	⅞ yard
Red for blocks	¼ yard	⅜ yard	⅜ yard
Blue for blocks	¼ yard	⅜ yard	⅜ yard
Backing	3⅜ yards*	5½ yards**	8 yards†
Binding	⅝ yard	¾ yard	⅞ yard
Batting	54" x 68"	73" x 93"	87" x 112"
On-point fusible interfacing	2¾ yards	3⅝ yards	6 yards
OR			
Straight-set fusible interfacing	2¼ yards	3½ yards	5¾ yards

* Two widths pieced horizontally
** Two widths pieced vertically
† Three widths pieced horizontally

CUTTING FOR LAP SIZE

All strips are cut across the width of the fabric.

Fabric	Number of 42"-Long Strips	Strip Width	Piece Length	Pieces
Darks	7	3⅜"	—	—
Mediums	7	3⅜"	—	—
	5	1¾"	—	—
Red	4	1⅛"	—	—
Blue	4	1⅛"	—	—
Background	8	1⅛"	—	—
	12	1¾"	—	—
	4	3"	3"	52
Inner border	5	2½"	—	—
Outer border	7	5½"	—	—
Binding	6	2½"	—	—
On-point interfacing	2	—	32 squares	—

CUTTING FOR TWIN SIZE

All strips are cut across the width of the fabric.

Fabric	Number of 42"-Long Strips	Strip Width	Piece Length	Pieces
Darks	8	4⅜"	—	—
Mediums	8	4⅜"	—	—
	6	2¼"	—	—
Red	5	1⅜"	—	—
Blue	5	1⅜"	—	—
Background	10	1⅜"	—	—
	14	2¼"	—	—
	6	4"	4"	52
Inner border	7	3"	—	—
Outer border	9	7"	—	—
Binding	9	2½"	—	—
Diagonal interfacing	2	–	42 squares	—

CUTTING FOR QUEEN SIZE

All strips are cut across the width of the fabric.

Fabric	Number of 42"-Long Strips	Strip Width	Piece Length	Pieces
Darks	10	5⅜"	—	—
Mediums	10	5⅜"	—	—
	7	2¾"	—	—
Red	6	1⅝"	—	—
Blue	6	1⅝"	—	—
Background	12	1⅝"	—	—
	17	2¾"	—	—
	7	5"	5"	52
Inner border	9	3"	—	—
Outer border	10	7"	—	—
Binding	10	2½"	—	—
On-point interfacing	2	–	72 squares	—

UNIT PIECING

1. With right sides together, sew red and blue strips to the background strips of the same width. Press seams toward the darker fabric. With right sides together, layer the strip sets in pairs as shown. Crosscut each pair of strips into segments the same width as the original strips.

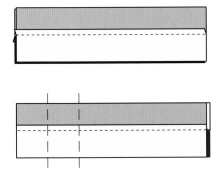

2. Chain piece the segments, making sure that the seams butt tightly together. Press seams and clip apart four-patch units.

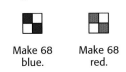

Make 68   Make 68
blue.   red.

3. Repeat steps 1 and 2, this time using medium strips and the wider background strips. Use the 1¾"-wide strips for the lap size, 2¼"-wide strips for the twin size, and 2¾"-wide strips for the queen size.

Make 48
assorted.

4. Cut the remaining background strips into squares. Join one small four-patch unit with one background square. Join sets to form units.

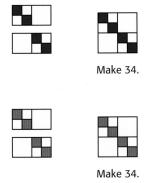

Make 34.

Make 34.

5. With right sides together, layer pairs of dark and medium strips that are the same width. Cut the strip pairs into squares. Cut the sets of squares in half diagonally.

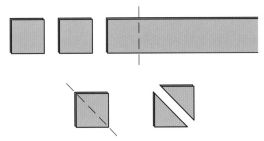

6. Chain piece the triangle pairs along the long edge. Press seams toward the darker fabric.

Make 140 units.

FAST-FORWARD PIECING ▶▶▶

1. Place the interfacing grid on your work surface, fusible side up. Following the master design for your quilt size on page 54, place the half-square-triangle units on the interfacing. Align the diagonal seam lines with the corners of the grid. Place the four-patch sections on the interfacing, aligning the seam lines within the units with the neighboring unit seam lines.

2. Fill in the remaining grid with squares as indicated on the quilt plan.

3. Evaluate your design. Make adjustments by replacing or rotating squares as needed.

4. Referring to "Quilt-Top Settings" on page 15, trim the background squares along the edges into setting triangles and triangle points. Place the triangles and triangle points on the grid.

5. Straighten the pieces on the grid. Fuse the pieces in place.

6. Fold and stitch the interfacing panel(s).

QUILT FINISHING

1. Refer to "Mitered Borders" on page 105 to measure and sew the border strips to the quilt top.

2. Layer the backing, batting, and quilt top; baste the layers together. Quilt as desired. Bind the quilt edges. See "Finishing Techniques," starting on page 104, for specific details on quilting and binding.

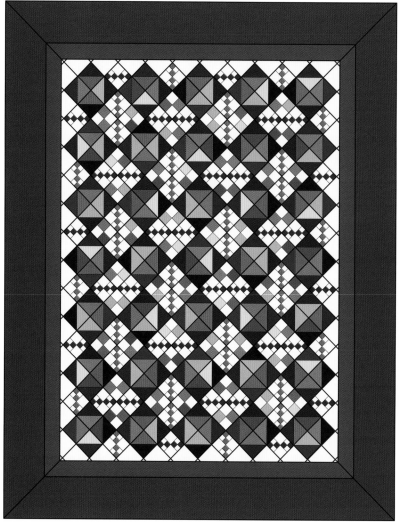

Quilt Plan

Hothouse Tulips

By Dina Pappas, 57½" x 57½". Rotating the Six Tulips blocks kept me intrigued with the unlimited layout possibilities. I settled on this diamond arrangement divided between hot and cool colors. The quilt shown here is the lap size.

QUILT FACTS

	Lap	Twin	Queen
Finished size	57½" x 57½"	66½" x 87½"	85½" x 85½"
Block set	4 x 4 straight	4 x 6 straight	6 x 6 straight
Total blocks	16	24	36
Finished block size	10½" x 10½"	10½" x 10½"	10½" x 10½"
Unfinished block size on interfacing	13" x 13"	13" x 13"	13" x 13"

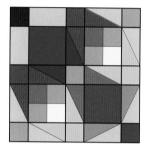

Hot House Tulips Block
Warm/Cool Variation

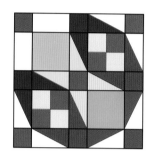

Hot House Tulips Block
Light/Dark Variation

Lap Master Design

Queen Master Design

Twin Master Design

MATERIALS

Yardage is based on 42"-wide fabric.

NOTE: Yardage and cutting directions for the lap and twin sizes use the warm-and-cool block variation, and the queen size uses the dark-and-light block variation. If you alter your quilt plan from these variations, adjust your fabric yardages accordingly.

	Lap	Twin	Queen
Outer border and binding	1¾ yards	1¾ yards	1¾ yards
Background	⅞ yard	1 yard	1½ yards
Greens for blocks	¾ yard	1 yard	¾ yard
Tan for blocks	—	—	⅝ yard
Dark yellow for blocks	½ yard	¾ yard	½ yard
Dark purple for blocks	½ yard	¾ yard	2¼ yards
Middle border	½ yard	1¾ yards	1⅞ yards
Dark blue for blocks	⅜ yard	½ yard	1 yard
Dark red for blocks	⅜ yard	½ yard	—
Light purple for blocks	¼ yard	¼ yard	—
Light yellow for blocks	¼ yard	¼ yard	½ yard
Light blue for blocks	¼ yard	⅜ yard	—
Medium red for blocks	¼ yard	⅜ yard	—
Dark pink for blocks	—	—	½ yard
Light pink for blocks	—	—	½ yard
Inner border	Included with background	⅞ yard	¾ yard
Backing	3⅞ yards*	5⅝ yards**	8¼ yards†
Batting	62" x 62"	71" x 92"	90" x 90"
Straight-set fusible interfacing	3 yards	3 yards	4½ yards

* Two widths pieced horizontally or vertically
** Two widths pieced vertically
† Three widths pieced horizontally or vertically

UNIT PIECING

1. For cutting instructions for your quilt size, refer to the charts on pages 62–64. Refer to block diagram as a color key. With right sides together, layer pairs of 4¼"-wide strips for tall triangle units. Cut the strip pairs into 2¼"-wide rectangles. Cut stacks of rectangles diagonally from corner to corner.

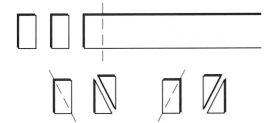

2. Trim tall triangles by using a template made with the pattern on page 31.

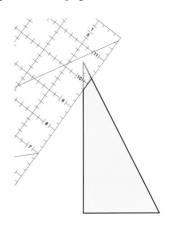

CUTTING FOR LAP SIZE

All strips are cut across the width of the fabric.

Fabric	Number of 42"-Long Strips	Strip Width	Piece Length	Pieces
Background	3	4¼"	—	—
	3	2"	3½"	32
	5	1½"	—	—
Dark purple	2	4¼"	—	—
	2	2"	2"	32
Light purple	2	2"	—	—
Dark yellow	2	4¼"	—	—
	2	2"	2"	32
Greens	1	4¼"	—	—
	3	2"	2"	48
	4	2"	—	—
Medium red	1	4¼"	—	—
Light blue	1	4¼"	—	—
Light yellow	2	2"	—	—
Dark red	2	3½"	3½"	16
	1	2"	2"	16
Dark blue	2	3½"	3½"	16
	1	2"	2"	16
Middle border	6	2"	—	—
Outer border	7	5½"	—	—
Binding	7	2½"	—	—
Interfacing	2	—	52"	—

3. Pair two tall triangles with right sides together and points facing in opposite directions. Line up the trimmed ends with the straight edges of the triangle. Chain piece the pairs. Press seams toward the dark fabric and clip apart the units. Trim the points.

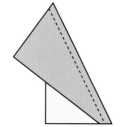

CUTTING FOR TWIN SIZE

All strips are cut across the width of the fabric.

Fabric	Number of 42"-Long Strips	Strip Width	Piece Length	Pieces
Background	5	4¼"	—	—
	5	2"	3½"	48
Dark purple	3	4¼"	—	—
	3	2"	2"	48
Light purple	3	2"	—	—
Dark yellow	3	4¼"	—	—
	3	2"	2"	48
Greens	2	4¼"	—	—
	4	2"	2"	72
	6	2"	—	—
Medium red	2	4¼"	—	—
Light blue	2	4¼"	—	—
Light yellow	3	2"	—	—
Dark red	3	3½"	3½"	24
	2	2"	2"	24
Dark blue	3	3½"	3½"	24
	2	2"	2"	24
Inner border	7	3½"	—	—
Middle border	8	2½"	—	—
Outer border	9	3½"	—	—
Binding	9	2½"	—	—
Interfacing	2	—	52"	—

4. Refer to the block diagram as a color key. With right sides together, join pairs of 2" strips for four-patch units. Press seams toward the darker fabric. With right sides together, layer a pair of strip sets and crosscut each pair into 2" segments. Chain piece the pairs, making sure that the seams butt tightly together. Press seams.

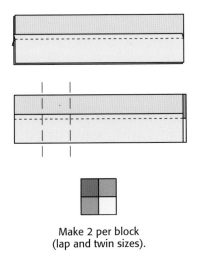

Make 2 per block
(lap and twin sizes).

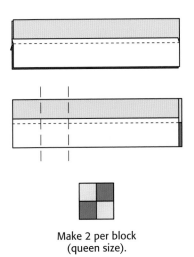

Make 2 per block
(queen size).

CUTTING FOR QUEEN SIZE

All strips are cut across the width of the fabric.

Fabric	Number of 42"-Long Strips	Strip Width	Piece Length	Pieces
Background	7	4¼"	—	—
	7	2"	3½"	72
Dark purple	9	4¼"	—	—
	8	2"	2"	144
Light yellow	3	4¼"	—	—
Light pink	3	4¼"	—	—
Greens	3	4¼"	—	—
	4	2"	2"	72
Tan	8	2"	—	—
Dark blue	6	2"	2"	108
	8	2"	—	—
Dark yellow	4	3½"	3½"	36
Dark pink	4	3½"	3½"	36
Inner border	8	2½"	—	—
Middle border	9	6½"	—	—
Outer border	10	3½"	—	—
Binding	9	2½"	—	—
Interfacing	2	—	78"	—

FAST-FORWARD PIECING ▶▶▶

1. Place the interfacing grid on your work surface, fusible side up. Following the master design for your quilt size on page 60, place tall triangle units on the interfacing. Align the diagonal seam lines as shown in "Tall Triangles" on page 31.

2. Place four-patch units on the interfacing, aligning the seam lines with the grid lines.

3. Fill in the remaining grid with squares as indicated on the quilt plan.

4. Evaluate your design. Make any adjustments by replacing or rotating squares as needed.

5. Straighten the pieces on the grid. Fuse the pieces in place.

6. Fold and stitch the interfacing panel(s).

QUILT FINISHING

1. Refer to "Mitered Borders" on page 105 to measure and sew the border strips to the quilt top.

2. Layer the backing, batting, and quilt top; baste the layers together. Quilt as desired. Bind the quilt edges. See "Finishing Techniques," starting on page 104, for details on quilting and binding.

Vintage Memories

By Dina Pappas, 76½" x 76½". Quilted by Judy Bolechala. Vivid burgundy adds sparkle to the gentle colors of this star quilt. This quilt plan could be further softened with the use of sashing. Take advantage of the fast-forward stitching lines and shade the divided sashing—darker near the posts, lighter in the center. Consider using softer colors in the Corner Star blocks to give a layered look. The quilt shown here is the lap size.

QUILT FACTS

	Wall Hanging	Lap	Queen
Finished size	52½" x 52½"	76½" x 76½"	88½" x 88½"
Block set	3 x 3 straight	5 x 5 straight	5 x 5 straight
Total blocks	5 Corner, 4 Memory	12 Corner, 13 Memory	12 Corner, 13 Memory
Finished block size	12" x 12"	12" x 12"	12" x 12"
Unfinished block size on interfacing	14½" x 14½"	14½" x 14½"	14½" x 14½"
Finished sashing width	–	–	2"
Sashing width on interfacing	–	–	2½"

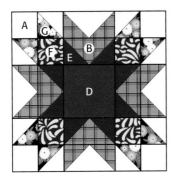

Memory Block

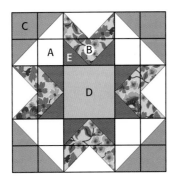

Corner Star Block

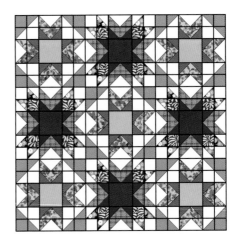

Wall-Hanging Master Design

Lap Master Design

Queen Master Design

MATERIALS

Yardage is based on 42"-wide fabric.

	Wall Hanging	Lap	Queen
Outer border	1¼ yards	1⅝ yards	2⅛ yards
Fabric A: Background	1 yard	2 yards	2 yards
Fabric B: Floral stars (total yardage)	¾ yard	1½ yards	1½ yards
Fabric C: Dark corners of Corner Star block	½ yard	¾ yard	¾ yard
Inner border	½ yard	⅝ yard	¾ yard
Fabric D: Block centers (total yardage)	⅜ yard	⅝ yard	⅝ yard
Fabric E: Small stars (total yardage)	⅜ yard	¾ yard	¾ yard
Fabric F: Memory block (total yardage)	¼ yard	⅜ yard	⅜ yard
Fabric G: Memory block (total yardage)	¼ yard	½ yard	½ yard
Sashing	—	—	¾ yard each of 3 fabrics (light, medium, medium-dark)
Posts (dark)	—	—	⅜ yard
Backing	3½ yards*	5 yards*	8½ yards**
Binding	⅝ yard	¾ yard	⅞ yard
Batting	57" x 57"	80" x 80"	93" x 93"
Straight-set fusible interfacing	1⅜ yards	4¼ yards	5 yards

* Two widths pieced horizontally or vertically
** Three widths pieced horizontally or vertically

CUTTING FOR WALL-HANGING SIZE

All strips are cut across the width of the fabric.

Fabric	Number of 42"-Long Strips	Strip Width	Piece Length	Pieces
Fabric A: Background	4	2⅞"	—	—
	3	2½"	2½"	36
	2	5¼"	5¼"	9
Fabric F: Memory block	1	2½"	2½"	16
Fabric G: Memory block	2	2⅞"	—	—
Fabric C: Corner Star block	2	2½"	2½"	20
	2	2⅞"	—	—
Fabric E: Small stars	3	2⅞"	2⅞"	36
Fabric B: Floral stars	2	5¼"	5¼"	9
	3	2⅞"	2⅞"	36
Fabric D: Block centers	2	4½"	4½"	9
Inner border	5	2½"	—	—
Outer border	6	6½"	—	—
Binding	6	2½"	—	—
Interfacing	1	43"	43"	—

CUTTING FOR LAP SIZE

All strips are cut across the width of the fabric.

Fabric	Number of 42"-Long Strips	Strip Width	Piece Length	Pieces
Fabric A: Background	8	2⅞"	—	—
	7	2½"	2½"	100
	4	5¼"	5¼"	25
Fabric F: Memory block	4	2½"	2½"	52
Fabric G: Memory block	4	2⅞"	—	—
Fabric C: Corner Star block	3	2½"	2½"	48
	4	2⅞"	—	—
Fabric E: Small stars	8	2⅞"	2⅞"	100
Fabric B: Floral stars	4	5¼"	5¼"	25
	8	2⅞"	2⅞"	100
Fabric D: Block centers	4	4½"	4½"	25
Inner border	7	2½"	—	—
Outer border	8	6½"	—	—
Binding	8	2½"	—	—
Interfacing	2	—	73"	—

CUTTING FOR QUEEN SIZE

All strips are cut across the width of the fabric.

Fabric	Number of 42"-Long Strips	Strip Width	Piece Length	Pieces
Fabric A: Background	8	2⅞"	—	—
	7	2½"	2½"	100
	4	5¼"	5¼"	25
Fabric F: Memory block	4	2½"	2½"	52
Fabric G: Memory block	4	2⅞"	—	—
Fabric C: Corner Star block	3	2½"	2½"	48
	4	2⅞"	—	—
Fabric E: Small stars	8	2⅞"	2⅞"	100
Fabric B: Floral stars	4	5¼"	5¼"	25
	8	2⅞"	2⅞"	100
Fabric D: Block centers	4	4½"	4½"	25
Sashing				
Light	8	2½"	4½"	60
Medium	8	2½"	2½"	120
Medium dark	8	2½"	2½"	120
Posts (dark)	3	2½"	2½"	36
Inner border	8	2½"	—	—
Outer border	10	6½"	—	—
Binding	10	2½"	—	—
Interfacing	2	—	88"	—

HALF-SQUARE-TRIANGLE UNIT PIECING

1. With right sides together, layer pairs of 2⅞" fabric A strips and 2⅞" fabric G strips. Cut strip pairs into 2⅞" squares. Cut sets of squares diagonally from corner to corner.

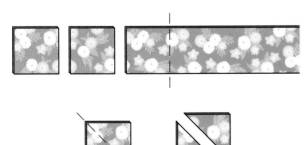

2. Chain piece the pairs along the long edge. Clip apart units and trim points.

Make 8
per Memory block.

3. Repeat for Corner Star block half-square-triangle units with 2⅞" fabric A strips and 2⅞" fabric C strips.

Make 8
per Corner Star block.

FLYING-GEESE UNIT PIECING

1. Fold half of the 2⅞" fabric E squares diagonally and press a crease or draw a diagonal line corner to corner. Trim ⅜" off the corner. Unfold the squares.

2. With right sides together, place two trimmed fabric E squares from step 1 on a 5¼" fabric B square. Make sure the diagonal creases align and the trimmed corners meet in the center. Sew ¼" away on both sides of the crease. Repeat for all 5¼" fabric B squares.

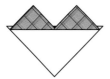

3. Cut on the center crease or line. Press seam allowances toward the small triangles. You now have two heart-shaped units.

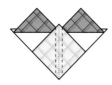

4. With right sides together, place a 2⅞" fabric E square on the fabric B triangle, with the diagonal line placed in the corner of the fabric B triangle. Sew ¼" away on both sides of the crease. Repeat for the second unit.

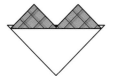

5. Cut on the center crease or line. Press the seam allowances toward the small triangles. Trim the points.

Make 4
per block.

6. Repeat for the 5¼" fabric A squares and the 2⅞" fabric B squares.

Make 4
per block.

FAST-FORWARD PIECING ⟩⟩⟩

1. Place the interfacing grid on your work surface, fusible side up. Following the master design for your quilt size on pages 66–67, place half-square-triangle units and flying-geese units on the interfacing. Align the diagonal seam lines with the corners of the grid.

2. Fill in the remaining grid with squares as indicated on the quilt plan.

3. For the queen-size quilt layout, add the sashing pieces.

4. Evaluate your design. Make any adjustments by replacing or rotating squares as needed.

5. Straighten the pieces on the grid. Fuse the pieces in place.

6. Fold and stitch the interfacing panel(s).

QUILT FINISHING

1. Refer to "Mitered Borders" on page 105 to measure and sew the border strips to the quilt top.

2. Layer the backing, batting, and quilt top; baste the layers together. Quilt as desired. Bind the quilt edges. See "Finishing Techniques," starting on page 104, for specific details on quilting and binding.

Layered Lattice

By Dina Pappas, 63" x 90". Quilted by Judy Bolechala. Alternating the posts on each row gives the lattice setting a woven look. This setting would be perfect for framing sampler blocks or a set of photo-transfer blocks. The quilt shown here is the twin size.

QUILT FACTS

	Lap	Twin	Queen
Finished size	63" x 63"	63" x 90"	90" x 90"
Block set	3 x 3 straight	3 x 5 straight	5 x 5 straight
Theme blocks	9	15	25
Finished block size	7½" x 7½"	7½" x 7½"	7½" x 7½"
Block size on interfacing	8" x 8"	8" x 8"	8" x 8"
Sashing units	24	38	60
Finished sashing size	6" x 7½"	6" x 7½"	6" x 7½"
Sashing size on interfacing	7½" x 8"	7½" x 8"	7½" x 8"
Posts	8 red, 8 green	12 red, 12 green	18 red, 18 green
Finished post size	6" x 6"	6" x 6"	6" x 6"
Unfinished post size on interfacing	7½" x 7½"	7½" x 7½"	7½" x 7½"

Layered Lattice
(Red)

Layered Lattice
(Green)

Lattice Sashing

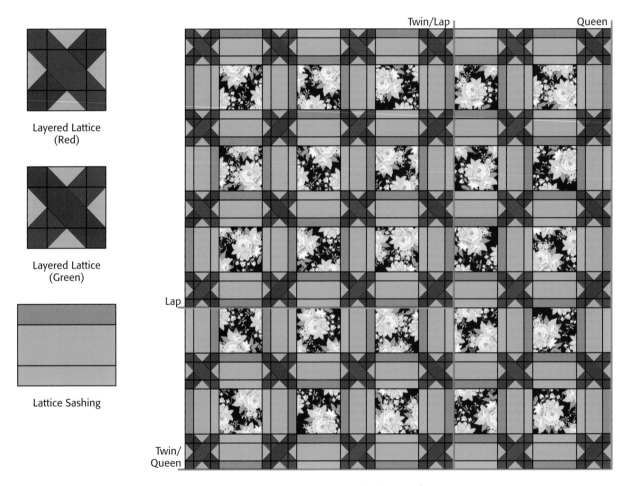

Master Design

MATERIALS

Yardage is based on 42"-wide fabric.

	Lap	Twin	Queen
Outer border	1½ yards	1⅞ yards	2⅛ yards
Background	⅞ yard	1⅜ yards	1⅞ yards
Theme blocks	⅝ yard	⅞ yard	1⅜ yards
Dark red for pieced blocks	⅝ yard	¾ yard	1 yard
Dark green for pieced blocks	⅝ yard	¾ yard	1 yard
Inner border	⅝ yard	⅝ yard	¾ yard
Light red for sashing	⅜ yard	⅝ yard	⅞ yard
Light green for sashing	⅜ yard	⅝ yard	⅞ yard
Backing	4 yards*	5¾ yards**	8½ yards†
Binding	⅝ yard	¾ yard	⅞ yard
Batting	67" x 67"	67" x 94"	94" x 94"
Straight-set fusible interfacing	3¼ yards	3¼ yards	5 yards

* Two widths pieced horizontally or vertically
** Two widths pieced vertically
† Three widths pieced horizontally or vertically

CUTTING FOR LAP SIZE

All strips are cut across the width of the fabric.

Fabric	Number of 42"-Long Strips	Strip Width	Piece Length	Pieces
Dark red and dark green	3 of each color	2"	2"	48 of each color
	2 of each color	2⅜"	2⅜"	32 of each color
	1 of each color	3½"	3½"	8 of each color
Background	2	4¼"	4¼"	16
	5	3½"	8"	24
Theme blocks	2	8"	8"	9
Light red and light green	5 of each color	2"	8"	24 of each color
Inner border	6	2½"	—	—
Outer border	7	6½"	—	—
Binding	7	2½"	—	—
Interfacing	2	—	54"	—

CUTTING FOR TWIN SIZE

All strips are cut across the width of the fabric.

Fabric	Number of 42"-Long Strips	Strip Width	Piece Length	Pieces
Dark red and dark green	4 of each color	2"	2"	72 of each color
	3 of each color	2⅜"	2⅜"	48 of each color
	2 of each color	3½"	3½"	12 of each color
Background	3	4¼"	4¼"	24
	8	3½"	8"	38
Theme blocks	3	8"	8"	15
Light red and light green	8 of each color	2"	8"	38 of each color
Inner border	7	2½"	—	—
Outer border	9	6½"	—	—
Binding	9	2½"	—	—
Interfacing	2	—	54"	—

CUTTING FOR QUEEN SIZE

All strips are cut across the width of the fabric.

Fabric	Number of 42"-Long Strips	Strip Width	Piece Length	Pieces
Dark red and dark green	6 of each color	2"	2"	108 of each color
	5 of each color	2⅜"	2⅜"	72 of each color
	2 of each color	3½"	3½"	18 of each color
Background	4	4¼"	4¼"	36
	12	3½"	8"	60
Theme blocks	5	8"	8"	25
Light red and light green	12 of each color	2"	8"	60 of each color
Inner border	9	2½"	—	—
Outer border	10	6½"	—	—
Binding	10	2½"	—	—
Interfacing	2	—	86"	—

FOLDED-SQUARE UNIT PIECING

1. Using the folded-square triangle technique, fold two 2" red squares in half diagonally. With right sides together, sew the squares to opposite corners of a 3½" green square. Trim seams and press triangles toward the middle.

2. Repeat using 2" green and 3½" red squares.

Make 1 per green block.   Make 1 per red block.

FLYING-GEESE UNIT PIECING

1. Fold all of the 2⅜" red squares diagonally and press a crease or draw a diagonal line from corner to corner. Trim ⅜" off a corner. Unfold squares.

⅜"

2. With right sides together, place two trimmed red squares on a 4¼" background square. Make sure the diagonal creases align and the trimmed corners meet in the middle. Sew ¼" away on both sides of the crease. Repeat for all of the 4¼" background squares.

3. Cut on the center crease or line. Press seam allowances toward the small triangles. You now have two heart-shaped units.

4. With right sides together, place a 2⅜" green square on the background triangle with the diagonal line placed in the corner of the background triangle. Sew ¼" away on both sides of the crease. Repeat for second heart-shaped unit.

5. Cut on the center crease or line. Press seam allowances toward the small triangles. Trim the points. Repeat to complete the flying-geese units.

Make 2 per block.   Make 2 per block.

FAST-FORWARD PIECING ⟫⟫

1. Place the interfacing grid on your work surface, fusible side up. Following the master design for your quilt size on page 72, place the folded-square units and flying-geese units on interfacing. Align the diagonal seam lines with the corners of the grid. Note that until sewn these diagonal seam lines will not meet each other.

2. Fill in the remaining grid with squares and rectangles as indicated on the quilt plan.

3. Evaluate your design. Make any adjustments by replacing or rotating squares as needed.

4. Straighten the pieces on the grid. Fuse the pieces in place.

5. Fold and stitch the interfacing panels.

QUILT FINISHING

1. Refer to "Mitered Borders" on page 105 to measure and sew the border strips to the quilt top.

2. Layer the backing, batting, and quilt top; baste the layers together. Quilt as desired. Bind the quilt edges. See "Finishing Techniques," starting on page 104, for details on quilting and binding.

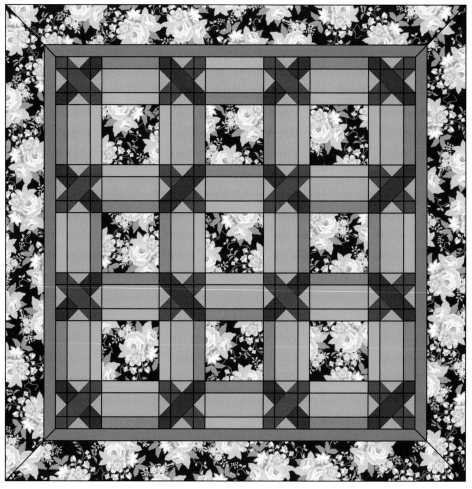

Lap Quilt Plan

Forget-Me-Not

By Dina Pappas, 51" x 61½". Quilted by Judy Bolechala. Judy's quilting helps distinguish the two light blue fabrics. The silver quilting thread lightens the floral fabric and strengthens the block design. The quilt shown here is the lap size.

QUILT FACTS

	Lap	Twin	Queen
Finished size	51" x 61½"	69" x 93"	85" x 97"
Block set	3 x 4 straight	4 x 6 straight	5 x 6 straight
Total blocks	12	24	30
Finished block size	10½" x 10½"	10½" x 10½"	10½" x 10½"
Unfinished block size on interfacing	12" x 12"	12" x 12"	12" x 12"
Finished sashing width	–	1½"	1½"
Sashing width on interfacing	–	2"	2"

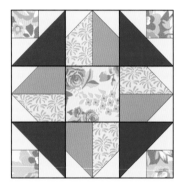

Forget-Me-Not Block

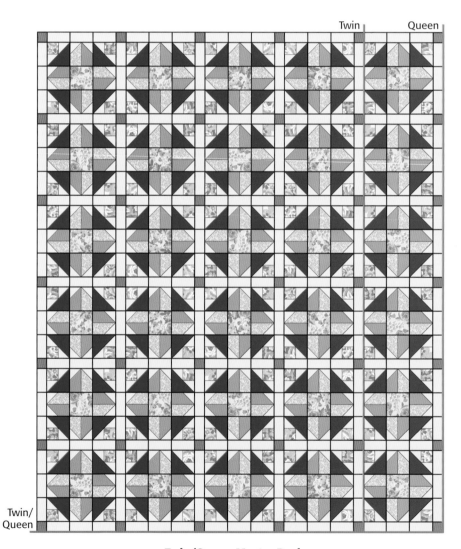

Twin/Queen Master Design

Lap Master Design

MATERIALS

Yardage is based on 42"-wide fabric.

	Lap	Twin	Queen
Large-scale floral for outer border and inset squares	1½ yards	2¼ yards	3⅛ yards
Blue floral for blocks and inner border	1 yard	1⅝ yards	1¾ yards
Background and sashing	¾ yard (no sashing)	2½ yards	3⅛ yards
Dark blue for blocks	⅝ yard	1 yard	1⅛ yards
Medium blue for blocks	½ yard	¾ yard	⅞ yard
Floral block centers	⅜ yard	½ yard	½ yard
Corner posts	—	¼ yard	¼ yard
Backing	3⅜ yards*	6 yards**	8⅛ yards†
Binding	⅝ yard	¾ yard	⅞ yard
Batting	55" x 66"	73" x 97"	89" x 101"
Straight-set fusible interfacing	1½ yards	3½ yards	4 yards

* Two widths pieced horizontally
** Two widths pieced vertically
† Three widths pieced horizontally

CUTTING FOR LAP SIZE

All strips are cut across the width of the fabric.

Fabric	Number of 42"-Long Strips	Strip Width	Piece Length	Pieces
Background	4	2¼"	3¼"	48
	6	2¼"	2¼"	96
Blue Floral	5	2¼"	4"	48
	4	4"	—	—
Medium blue	5	2¼"	4"	48
Large-scale floral	3	2¼"	2¼"	48
	6	6½"	—	—
Dark blue	3	4"	5"	24
	1	4"	4"	4
Floral block centers	2	4"	4"	12
Binding	7	2½"	—	—
Interfacing	1	36"	48"	—

CUTTING FOR TWIN SIZE

All strips are cut across the width of the fabric.

Fabric	Number of 42"-Long Strips	Strip Width	Piece Length	Pieces
Background	8	2¼"	3¼"	96
	12	2¼"	2¼"	192
	18	2"	4"	174
Blue floral	10	2¼"	4"	96
	7	4"	—	—
Medium blue	10	2¼"	4"	96
Large-scale floral	6	2¼"	2¼"	96
	9	6½"	—	—
Dark blue	6	4"	5"	48
	1	4"	4"	4
Floral block centers	3	4"	4"	24
Posts	2	2"	2"	35
Binding	9	2½"	—	—
Interfacing	2	—	58"	—

CUTTING FOR QUEEN SIZE

All strips are cut across the width of the fabric.

Fabric	Number of 42"-Long Strips	Strip Width	Piece Length	Pieces
Background	10	2¼"	3¼"	120
	15	2¼"	2¼"	240
	22	2"	4"	213
Blue Floral	12	2¼"	4"	120
	7	4"	—	—
Medium blue	12	2¼"	4"	120
Large-scale floral	8	2¼"	2¼"	120
	10	8½"	—	—
Dark blue	8	4"	5"	60
	1	4"	4"	4
Floral centers	3	4"	4"	30
Posts	3	2"	2"	42
Binding	10	2½"	—	—
Interfacing	2	—	72"	—

FOLDED-SQUARE UNIT PIECING

1. With right sides together, use the folded-square technique to sew a 2¼" background square to a 2¼" x 4" blue floral rectangle. Sew a 2¼" background square to a 2¼" x 4" medium blue rectangle, angling the seam in the opposite direction from the first unit.

2. With right sides together, sew the pieced rectangles together. Note that the angled seams will butt together. Press the seam open.

Make 4
per block.

INSET-SQUARE UNIT PIECING

1. With right sides together, sew a 2¼" x 3¼" background rectangle to a 2¼" inset square. Repeat. Sew two units together as shown. In the middle of the unit, clip the seam allowance so that you can press the seams on either side toward the rectangles.

Make 2 per block.

Clip.

2. With right sides together, place the pieced unit from step 1 on a 4" x 5" dark blue rectangle. Align the 45° line on a ruler with the edge of the rectangles and cut them apart, leaving a ¼" seam allowance beyond the sewn corners.

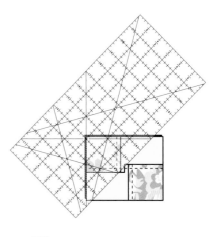

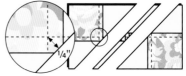

Cut apart units,
leaving ¼" seam allowance.

3. Sew the units together. Press the seam allowance toward the large triangle.

Make 4
per block.

FAST-FORWARD PIECING ⟫⟫⟫

1. Place the interfacing grid on your work surface, fusible side up. Following the master design for your quilt size on page 78, place folded-square units and inset-square units on the interfacing. Align the diagonal seam lines with the corners of the grid.

2. Fill in the remaining grid with squares as indicated on the quilt plan. Lap and queen quilts will also have rectangles for sashing.

3. Evaluate your design. Make any adjustments by replacing or rotating squares as needed.

4. Straighten the pieces on the grid. Fuse the pieces in place.

5. Fold and stitch the interfacing panels.

QUILT FINISHING

1. Refer to "Borders with Corner Squares" on page 104 to measure and sew the blue floral inner-border strips and dark blue 4" corner squares to the quilt top. Refer to "Mitered Borders" on page 105 to measure and sew the outer-border strips to the quilt top.

2. Layer the backing, batting, and quilt top; baste the layers together. Quilt as desired. Bind the quilt edges. See "Finishing Techniques," starting on page 104, for details on quilting and binding.

Lap Quilt Plan

By Dina Pappas, 52½" x 70½". Quilted by Judy Bolechala. One simple triangle shape in different sizes produces a pleasing repeat pattern. The quilt shown here is the lap size.

QUILT FACTS

	Wall Hanging	Twin	Queen
Finished size	52½" x 70½"	70½" x 88½"	88½" x 88½"
Block set	4 x 6 straight	6 x 8 straight	8 x 8 straight
Total blocks	24	48	64
Finished block size	9" x 9"	9" x 9"	9" x 9"
Unfinished block size on interfacing	10" x 10"	10" x 10"	10" x 10"

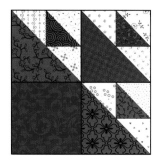

Formation Flying Block

Lap/Twin Master Design

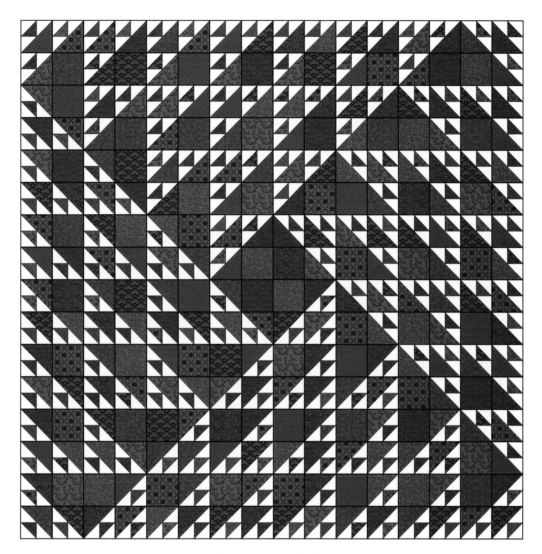

Queen Master Design

MATERIALS

Yardage is based on 42"-wide fabric.

	Lap	Twin	Queen
Darks for blocks (total yardage)	1¾ yards	3⅜ yards	4½ yards
Outer border	1½ yards	1⅞ yards	2⅛ yards
Background for blocks (total yardage)	1⅛ yards	2 yards	2½ yards
Inner border	⅝ yard	¾ yard	¾ yard
Backing	3½ yards*	5⅝ yards**	8½ yards†
Binding	⅝ yard	¾ yard	¾ yard
Batting	57" x 75"	75" x 93"	93" x 93"
Straight-set fusible interfacing	1¾ yards	3½ yards	4½ yards

* Two widths pieced horizontally
** Two widths pieced vertically
† Three widths pieced horizontally or vertically

CUTTING FOR LAP SIZE

All strips are cut across the width of the fabric.

Fabric	Number of 42"-Long Strips	Strip Width	Piece Length	Pieces
Background	3	3⅛"	—	—
	8	2¾"	3¾"	72
Darks	3	3⅛"	—	—
	6	5"	6"	36
	3	5"	5"	24
Inner border	6	2½	—	—
Outer border	7	6½"	—	—
Binding	7	2½"	—	—
Interfacing	1	—	60"	—

CUTTING FOR TWIN SIZE

All strips are cut across the width of the fabric.

Fabric	Number of 42"-Long Strips	Strip Width	Piece Length	Pieces
Background	6	3⅛"	—	—
	15	2¾"	3¾"	144
Darks	6	3⅛"	—	—
	12	5"	6"	72
	6	5"	5"	48
Inner border	8	2½"	—	—
Outer border	9	6½"	—	—
Binding	9	2½"	—	—
Interfacing	2	—	60"	—

CUTTING FOR QUEEN SIZE

All strips are cut across the width of the fabric.

Fabric	Number of 42"-Long Strips	Strip Width	Piece Length	Pieces
Backgrounds	8	3⅛"	—	—
	20	2¾"	3¾"	192
Darks	8	3⅛"	—	—
	16	5"	6"	96
	8	5"	5"	64
Inner border	8	2½"	—	—
Outer border	10	6½"	—	—
Binding	10	2½"	—	—
Interfacing	2	—	80"	—

INSET-TRIANGLE UNIT PIECING

1. With right sides together, layer pairs of 3⅛" background strips and 3⅛" dark strips. Cut strip pairs into 3⅛" squares. Cut sets of squares diagonally from corner to corner.

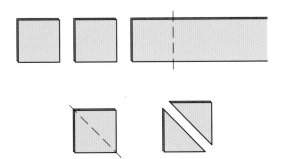

2. Chain piece the triangle pairs along the long edge. Press seams toward the dark fabric.

Make 3
per block.

3. With right sides together, sew a 2¾" x 3¾" background rectangle to a half-square-triangle unit, referring to diagram for proper placement and angle of seam. Repeat. Sew two units together. In the middle of each unit, clip the seam allowance through the stitching line so that you can press the seams on either side toward the rectangles.

Clip.

4. With right sides together, place the pieced unit from step 3 on a 5" x 6" dark rectangle. Align the 45° line on the ruler with the edge of the

rectangles and cut them apart, leaving a ¼" seam allowance beyond the sewn corners.

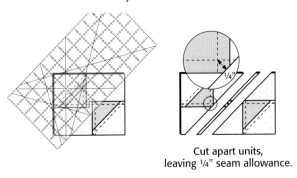

Cut apart units,
leaving ¼" seam allowance.

5. Sew the units. Press seam allowances toward the large triangles.

Make 3 per block.

FAST-FORWARD PIECING ⟫⟫

1. Place the interfacing grid on your work surface, fusible side up. Following the master design for your quilt size on pages 84–85, place inset-triangle units on the interfacing. Align the unit diagonal seam lines with the lines and corners of the grid.

2. Fill in the remaining grid with squares as indicated on the quilt plan.

3. Evaluate your design. Make any adjustments by replacing or rotating squares as needed.

4. Straighten the pieces on the grid. Fuse the pieces in place.

5. Fold and stitch the interfacing panels.

QUILT FINISHING

1. Refer to "Mitered Borders" on page 105 to measure and sew the border strips to the quilt top.

2. Layer the backing, batting, and quilt top; baste the layers together. Quilt as desired. Bind the quilt edges. See "Finishing Techniques," starting on page 104, for details on quilting and binding.

Berry Patch Baskets

By Dina Pappas, 82" x 96⅞". Quilted by Deb Cadwallender. The four-patch unit in the Basket Patch block develops interesting secondary designs when rotated. The quilt shown here is the queen size.

QUILT FACTS

	Lap	**Twin**	**Queen**
Finished size	52¼" x 67⅛"	67⅛" x 82"	82" x 96⅞"
Block set	2 x 3 diagonal	3 x 4 diagonal	4 x 5 diagonal
Total blocks	8	18	32
Finished block size	10½" x 10½"	10½" x 10½"	10½" x 10½"
Unfinished block size on interfacing	12" x 12"	12" x 12"	12" x 12"

Berry Patch Basket Block

Lap Master Design

Queen Master Design

Twin Master Design

MATERIALS

Yardage is based on 42"-wide fabric.

	Lap	Twin	Queen
Background	1⅜ yards	2⅜ yards	3⅝ yards
Gold border background	¾ yard	1 yard	1⅛ yard
Basket center square	¼ yard	⅜ yard	⅝ yard
Yellow for blocks	¼ yard	¼ yard	¼ yard
Red for blocks	¼ yard	¼ yard	⅜ yard
Purple for blocks	¼ yard	⅜ yard	½ yard
Green for blocks	⅜ yard	⅝ yard	⅞ yard
Assorted colors for four-patch units and border triangles (total yardage)	⅝ yard	1 yard	1⅛ yards
Inner border	½ yard	⅝ yard	¾ yard
Outer border	1½ yards	1⅝ yards	2⅛ yards
Binding	⅝ yard	¾ yard	⅞ yard
Batting	57" x 71"	71" x 86"	86" x 101"
Backing	3½ yards*	5¼ yards**	7⅞ yards†
On-point fusible interfacing	2 yards	4 yards	6 yards
OR			
Straight-set interfacing	2½ yards	4¼ yards	6½ yards

* Two widths pieced horizontally
** Two widths pieced vertically
† Three widths pieced horizontally

FOUR-PATCH UNIT PIECING

1. For cutting instructions for your quilt size, refer to the charts on pages 91–93. With right sides together, layer 2⅝" background strips and 2⅝" red strips. Cut strips into 2⅝" squares. Cut the sets of squares diagonally from corner to corner. Chain piece the pairs along the long edge. Press seams toward the dark fabric.

Make 2
per block.

2. Sew a 2¼" background square to a half-square-triangle unit from step 1. Sew a yellow 2¼" square to a half-square-triangle unit from step 1. Refer to diagram for proper placement of seams. Sew together to form a unit. Press seam in either direction.

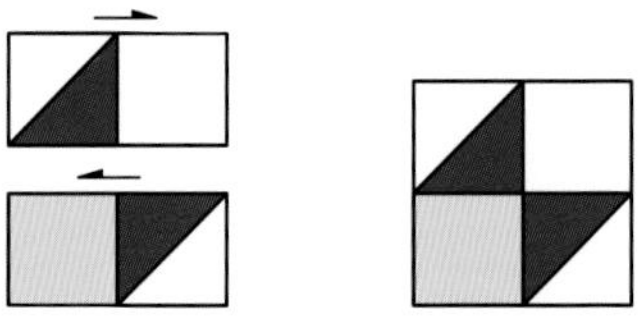

Make 1
per block.

CUTTING FOR LAP SIZE

All strips are cut across the width of the fabric.

Fabric	Number of 42"-Long Strips	Strip Width	Piece Length	Pieces
Background	1	2⅝"	—	—
	1	2¼"	2¼"	8
	1	4¾"	4¾"	5
	6	4"	4"	54
	2	4⅜"	4⅜"	13
Red	1	2⅝"	—	—
Yellow	1	2¼"	2¼"	8
Assorted colors	—	2¼"	2¼"	32
	—	4⅜"	4⅜"	13
	—	4¾"	4¾"	2
Purple	2	2⅝"	2⅝"	16
Green	1	2¼"	2¼"	16
	2	2¼"	4"	16
Gold border background	4	4"	4"	38
	1	4¾"	4¾"	1
Basket center square	1	4"	4"	8
Inner border	5	2½"	—	—
Outer border	7	6½"	—	—
Binding	7	2½"	—	—
On-point interfacing	1	—	44 squares	—

3. Sew two 2¼" assorted-color squares together into a pair. Press seam to one side. Repeat with another two 2¼" colored squares. Press seam to the opposite side. Join pairs, butting seams tightly together. Press seam in either direction.

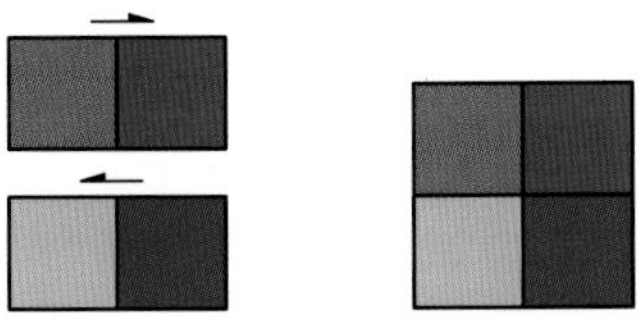

Make 1
per block.

FLYING-GEESE UNIT PIECING

1. Fold all of the 2⅝" purple squares diagonally and press a crease or draw a diagonal line from corner to corner. Set aside half of the marked squares for step 4. Trim ⅜" off a corner of each remaining marked square as shown. Unfold squares.

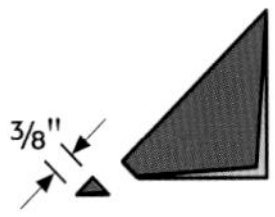

CUTTING FOR TWIN SIZE

All strips are cut across the width of the fabric.

Fabric	Number of 42"-Long Strips	Strip Width	Piece Length	Pieces
Background	2	2⅝"		
	2	2¼"	2¼"	18
	2	4¾"	4¾"	10
	11	4"	4"	106
	3	4⅜"	—	—
Red	2	2⅝"	—	—
Yellow	2	2¼"	2¼"	18
Assorted colors	—	2¼"	2¼"	72
	—	4⅜"	4⅜"	19
	—	4¾"	4¾"	2
Purple	3	2⅝"	2⅝"	36
Green	3	2¼"	2¼"	36
	4	2¼"	4"	36
Gold border background	5	4"	4"	50
	1	4¾"	4¾"	1
Basket center square	2	4"	4"	18
Inner border	7	2½"	—	—
Outer border	8	6½"	—	—
Binding	8	2½"	—	—
On-point interfacing	2	—	44 squares	—

2. With right sides together, place two trimmed purple squares on a 4¾" background square. Make sure the diagonal creases align and the trimmed corners meet in the center. Sew ¼" away on both sides of the crease. Repeat, using the remaining 4¾" background squares but leaving one square to use for corner units.

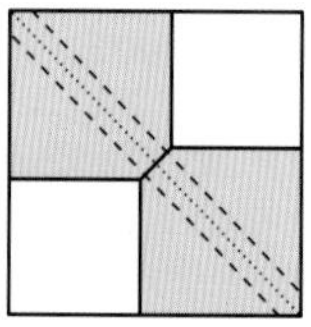

3. Cut on the center crease or line. Press seam allowances toward the small triangles. You now have two heart-shaped units.

4. With right sides together, place a 2⅝" purple square on the background triangle with the diagonal line placed in the corner of the background triangle. Sew ¼" away on both sides of the crease. Repeat for second unit.

5. Cut on the center crease or line. Press seam allowances toward the small triangles. Trim the seam allowance points.

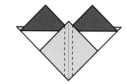

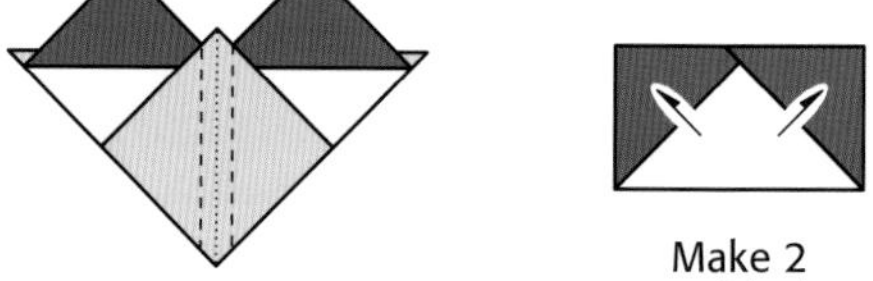

Make 2
per block.

CUTTING FOR QUEEN SIZE

All strips are cut across the width of the fabric.

Fabric	Number of 42"-Long Strips	Strip Width	Piece Length	Pieces
Background	3	2⅝"	—	—
	2	2¼"	2¼"	32
	3	4¾"	4¾"	17
	18	4"	4"	174
	3	4⅜"	4⅜"	25
Red	3	2⅝"	—	—
Yellow	2	2¼"	2¼"	32
Assorted colors	—	2¼"	2¼"	128
	—	4⅜"	4⅜"	25
	—	4¾"	4¾"	2
Purple	5	2⅝"	2⅝"	64
Green	4	2¼"	2¼"	64
	7	2¼"	4"	64
Gold border background	6	4"	4"	62
	1	4¾"	4¾"	1
Basket center square	4	4"	4"	32
Inner border	8	2½"	—	—
Outer border	10	6½"	—	—
Binding	10	2½"	—	—
On-point interfacing	2	—	68 squares	—

6. Join the flying-geese units to 2¼" x 4" green rectangles to form a unit.

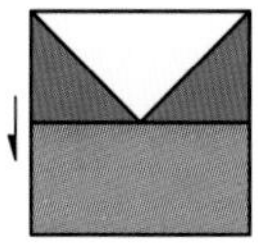

Make 2
per block.

FOLDED-CORNER UNIT PIECING

With right sides together, use the folded-square technique to sew a 2¼" green square to a 4" background square. Trim excess and press seam toward the green triangle.

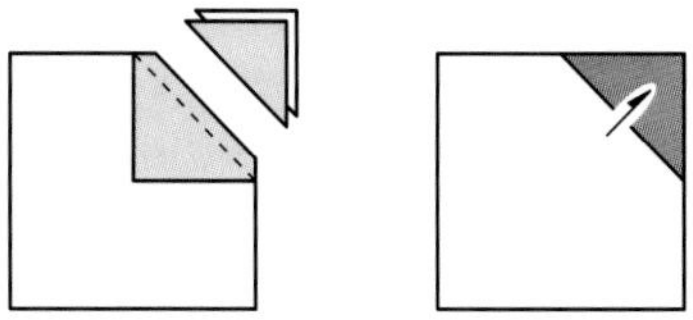

Make 2
per block.

BORDER UNIT PIECING

1. With right sides together, place the 4⅜" background squares on the 4⅜" assorted color squares. Cut sets in half diagonally. Chain piece the triangle pairs along the long edge. Press seams toward the colored triangles.

Border Unit
Lap: Make 26.
Twin: Make 38.
Queen: Make 50.

2. With right sides together, place one 4¾" gold square on one 4¾" assorted color square. Cut squares diagonally from corner to corner. Repeat with a remaining 4¾" assorted-color square and a 4¾" background square. Chain piece the triangle pairs along the long edge.

3. With right sides together, place one gold unit on one background unit, butting diagonal seams together. Cut corner to corner, perpendicular to the seam line. Piece the pairs together along the long edge. Press seam in either direction.

Make 4
corner units.

4. Reserve four 4" gold border squares. Refer to "Quilt-Top Settings" on page 15 to trim the remaining 4" gold border squares into setting triangle units and setting points. Use small trimmed corners as filler triangles for the ¼" seam allowance along the pieced border. Use reserved squares to fill in the corners.

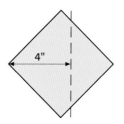

4"

Trim setting squares.

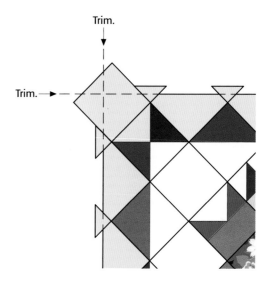

Trim.

Trim.

FAST-FORWARD PIECING ⟫⟫⟫

1. Place the interfacing grid on your work surface, fusible side up. Following the master design for your quilt size on page 89, place four-patch units, flying-geese units, and folded-corner units on the interfacing. Align the diagonal seam lines with the corners and lines of the grid.

2. Fill in the remaining grid with squares as indicated on the quilt plan.

3. Evaluate your design. Make any adjustments by replacing or rotating squares as needed.

4. Straighten the pieces on the grid. Fuse the pieces in place.

5. Fold and stitch the interfacing panels.

QUILT FINISHING

1. Refer to "Mitered Borders" on page 105 to measure and sew the border strips to the quilt top.

2. Layer the backing, batting, and quilt top; baste the layers together. Quilt as desired. Bind the quilt edges. See "Finishing Techniques," starting on page 104, for details on quilting and binding.

Lap Quilt Plan

Home in the Pines

By Dina Pappas, 57" x 75½". Rome wasn't built in a day but this neighborhood was. The homes were constructed, and all of the trees grew, in one afternoon. The borders allowed me time for a longer visit before moving on to other quilts. The quilt shown here is the lap size.

QUILT FACTS

	Lap	Twin	Queen
Finished size	57" x 75½"	75" x 92½"	92½" x 92½"
Block set	3 x 5 straight	5 x 7 straight	7 x 7 straight
House blocks	8	18	25
Pine blocks	7	17	24
Finished block size	9" x 9"	9" x 9"	9" x 9"
Unfinished block size on interfacing	10" x 10½"	10" x 10½"	10" x 10½"

House Block

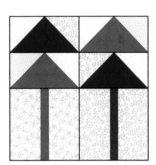

Pines Block

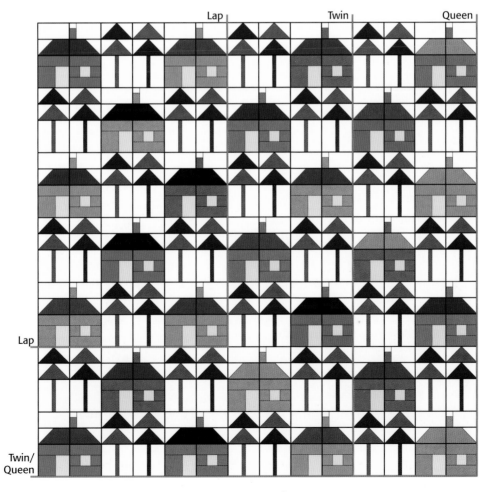

Master Design

MATERIALS

Yardage is based on 42"-wide fabric.

	Lap	Twin	Queen
Outer border	1⅜ yards	1¾ yards	1⅞ yards
Background for blocks and inner border	1½ yards	2½ yards	3⅛ yards
Light green background for pieced border	⅞ yard	1⅛ yards	1⅜ yards
Purple borders	⅞ yard	1⅛ yards	1¼ yards
Assorted colors for pieced border	⅝ yard	⅝ yard	¾ yard
Tree tops (total yardage)	½ yard	⅝ yard	¾ yard
Houses (total yardage)	½ yard	⅞ yard	1¼ yards
Yellow for doors and windows	¼ yard	⅜ yard	½ yard
Roofs	¼ yard	½ yard	¾ yard
Tree trunks (total yardage)	⅛ yard	¼ yard	¼ yard
Binding	⅝ yard	¾ yard	⅞ yard
Batting	62" x 79"	79" x 97"	97" x 97"
Backing	3¾ yards*	6 yards**	9 yards†
Straight-set interfacing	1½ yards	3 yards	4 yards
On-point interfacing for border	2 yards	2¾ yards	2⅞ yards
OR			
Straight-set interfacing for border	1¼ yards	2 yards	2⅛ yards

* Two widths pieced horizontally
** Two widths pieced vertically
† Three widths pieced horizontally or vertically

PINE UNIT PIECING

1. For cutting instructions for your quilt size, refer to the charts on pages 99–101. Fold all of the 3⅛" background squares diagonally and press a crease or draw a diagonal line from corner to corner. Set aside half of the marked squares for step 4. Trim ⅜" off a corner of the remaining squares as shown. Unfold squares.

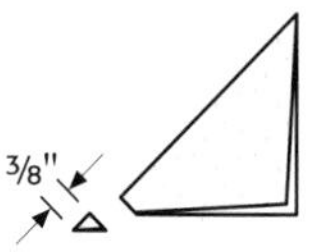

2. With right sides together, place two trimmed background squares on a 5¾" tree top square. Make sure the diagonal creases align and the trimmed corners meet in the center. Sew ¼" away on both sides of the crease. Repeat with the remaining 3⅛" background squares and 5¾" tree top squares.

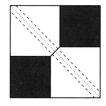

3. Cut on the center crease or line. Press seam allowances toward the small triangles. You now have two heart-shaped units.

CUTTING FOR LAP SIZE

All strips are cut across the width of the fabric.

Fabric	Number of 42"-Long Strips	Strip Width	Piece Length	Pieces
Background	3	3⅛"	3⅛"	28
	4	2½"	5"	28
	1	1¼"	1½"	8
	1	2¾"	4"	8
	2	2¾"	2¾"	16
	1	2¾"	5"	8
Top and bottom background borders	2	2½"	—	—
Side background borders	3	2¼"	—	—
Tree tops	2	5¾"	5¾"	7
Tree trunks	2	1"	5"	14
Houses	1	1½"	2"	8
	1	3"	3½"	8
	3	2"	5"	24
	1	2"	2"	16
Roofs	2	2¾"	5"	16
Yellow	1	2½"	3½"	8
	1	2"	2"	8
Purple borders	10	2½"	—	—
Assorted colors for pieced border	5	3"	3"	54
Light green	9	3"	3"	116
Outer border	7	6"	—	—
Binding	7	2½"	—	—
Interfacing for blocks	1	—	53"	—

4. With right sides together, place a 3⅛" background square on the tree triangle, with the diagonal line placed in the corner of the tree triangle. Sew ¼" away on both sides of the crease. Repeat for second unit.

5. Cut on the center crease or line. Press seam allowances toward the small triangles. Trim the points.

Make 4
per Tree block.

6. Sew a 2½" x 5" background rectangle to each side of a 1" x 5" tree trunk rectangle. Press seams toward the tree trunk.

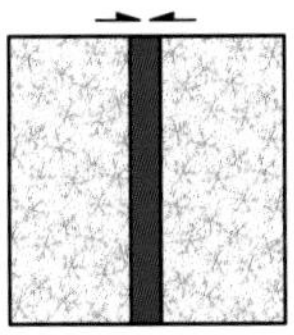

Make 2
per Tree block.

CUTTING FOR TWIN SIZE

All strips are cut across the width of the fabric.

Fabric	Number of 42"-Long Strips	Strip Width	Piece Length	Pieces
Background	6	3⅛"	3⅛"	68
	9	2½"	5"	72
	1	1¼"	1½"	18
	2	2¾"	4"	18
	3	2¾"	2¾"	36
	3	2¾"	5"	18
Top and bottom background borders	3	2"	—	—
Side background borders	4	2¼"	—	—
Tree tops	3	5¾"	5¾"	17
Tree trunks	5	1"	5"	34
Houses	1	1½"	2"	18
	2	3"	3½"	18
	7	2"	5"	54
	2	2"	2"	36
Roofs	5	2¾"	5"	36
Yellow	2	2½"	3½"	18
	1	2"	2"	18
Purple borders	13	2½"	—	—
Assorted colors for pieced border	6	3"	3"	74
Light green	12	3"	3"	156
Outer border	9	6"	—	—
Binding	10	2½"	—	—
Interfacing for blocks	2	—	50"	—

HOUSE UNIT PIECING

1. With right sides together, sew a 1¼" x 1½" background rectangle to a 1½" x 2" house rectangle. Press seam toward the house. Sew unit to a 2¾" x 4" background rectangle. Press seam in either direction.

Make 1
per House block.

2. With right sides together, use the folded-square technique to sew a 2¾" background square to a 2¾" x 5" roof rectangle. Trim seam and press toward background triangle. Stitch another unit, with the background square sewn onto the opposite end of the roof rectangle.

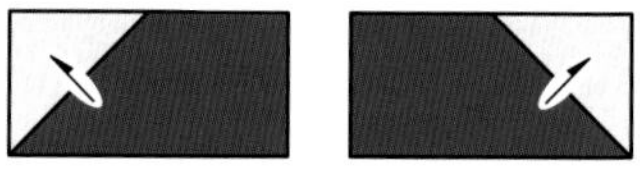

Make 1 each per House block.

CUTTING FOR QUEEN SIZE

All strips are cut across the width of the fabric.

Fabric	Number of 42"-Long Strips	Strip Width	Piece Length	Pieces
Background	8	3⅛"	3⅛"	96
	12	2½"	5"	96
	4	2¾"	5"	25
	4	2¾"	2¾"	50
	1	1¼"	1½"	25
	3	2¾"	4"	25
	7	2"	—	—
Tree tops	4	5¾"	5¾"	24
Tree trunks	6	1"	5"	48
Houses	2	1½"	2"	25
	3	3"	3½"	25
	10	2"	5"	75
	3	2"	2"	50
Roofs	7	2¾"	5"	50
Yellow	3	2½"	3½"	25
	2	2"	2"	25
Purple borders	15	2½"	—	—
Assorted colors for pieced border	7	3"	3"	84
Light green	14	3"	3"	176
Outer border	10	6"	—	—
Binding	10	2½"	—	—
Interfacing for blocks	2	—	70"	—

3. With right sides together, sew a 3" x 3½" house rectangle to a 2½" x 3½" yellow rectangle. Press seam toward the house. With right sides together, sew a 2" x 5" house rectangle to the previous unit. The yellow rectangle will be on the right. Press seam toward the house rectangle.

Make 1
per House block.

4. With right sides together, sew a 2" house square to each side of a 2" yellow square. Press seams toward the house squares. Sew a 2" x 5" house rectangle to the top and bottom to complete the unit along the long edges. Press seams toward the house rectangles.

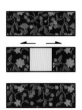

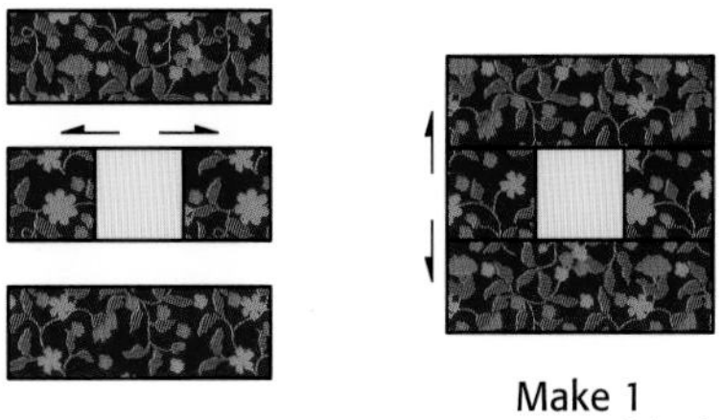

Make 1
per House block.

FAST-FORWARD PIECING ►►►

1. Place the interfacing grid on your work surface, fusible side up. Following the master design for your quilt size on page 97, place the tree units and roof units on the interfacing. Align the diagonal seam lines with the corners and lines of the grid.

2. Fill in the remaining grid with squares as indicated on the quilt plan.

3. Evaluate your design. Make any adjustments by replacing or rotating squares as needed.

4. Straighten the pieces on the grid. Fuse the pieces in place.

5. Fold and stitch the interfacing panels.

BORDER UNIT PIECING

1. Refer to "Straight-Cut Borders" on page 104 to measure and sew the inner borders to the quilt top. Be sure to use the proper strip widths for the top, bottom, and side borders as noted in the cutting charts.

2. Refer to "Straight-Cut Borders" on page 104 to measure and sew the first purple borders to the quilt top.

3. Place the interfacing grid for the pieced border on your work surface, fusible side up. Following the master design below for your quilt size, place 3" border squares on the interfacing.

4. Refer to "Quilt-Top Settings" on page 15 to trim the corners of 3" light green border squares 3" from a corner. Use small trimmed corners as filler triangles for the ¼" seam allowance along the pieced border.

Trim side squares.

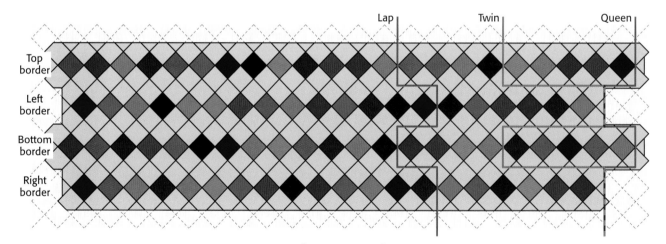

Border Master Design

5. Straighten the pieces on the grid. Fuse the pieces in place.

6. Fold and stitch the interfacing panels.

7. Centering the dark squares, cut 4" border strips. Be sure that you have a ¼" seam allowance beyond the corners of the dark squares.

8. Sew the side borders to the quilt first and then add the top and bottom borders. Press seams toward the purple borders.

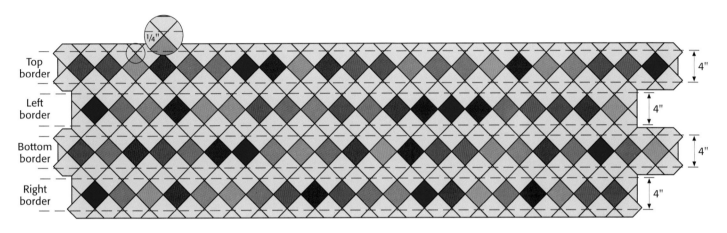

QUILT FINISHING

1. Refer to "Straight-Cut Borders" on page 104 to measure and sew the remaining purple and outer border strips to the quilt top.

2. Layer the backing, batting, and quilt top; baste the layers together. Quilt as desired. Bind the quilt edges. See "Finishing Techniques," starting on page 104, for details on quilting and binding.

Twin Quilt Plan

Finishing Techniques

Congratulations! You've fast-forwarded your quilt to the finishing stage. The final steps are done traditionally. Here are the basics, including adding borders and binding, to help you complete your project.

ADDING BORDERS

Once your units are fused onto the interfacing, you are ready to make your border choices. I prefer to see the final quilt layout before choosing the border fabric, so that I can balance the color in the quilt. For example, if one color dominates the quilt, you may want to avoid adding more in the border. You could pull another color out of the quilt top for the inner border and then use your favorite fabric for an outer border. Many people use their focus fabric for the outer border to help give a cohesive look to the quilt.

Many of the quilts in the book call for plain border strips. These strips are cut across the width of the fabric and are then seamed together. Then individual border lengths are cut from these strips.

Straight-Cut Borders

1. Measure the quilt top vertically at the center from raw edge to raw edge. Cut two border strips to that measurement. Mark the centers of the border strips and the centers along the sides of the quilt, matching ends and centers and easing, if necessary. Press the seam allowances toward the borders.

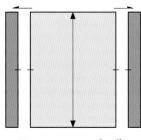

Measure center of quilt, top to bottom. Mark centers.

2. Measure the quilt top horizontally at the center from raw edge to raw edge, including the border pieces just added. Cut two border strips to that measurement. Mark the centers of the border strips and the centers of the top and bottom of the quilt top. Join the border strips to the top and bottom of the quilt, matching ends and centers and easing, if necessary. Press the seam allowances toward the borders.

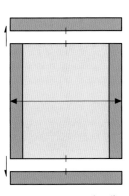

Measure center of quilt, side to side, including borders. Mark centers.

Borders with Corner Squares

1. Measure the quilt top vertically at the center from raw edge to raw edge. Cut two border strips to that measurement. Measure the quilt top horizontally at the center from raw edge to raw edge. Cut two border strips to that measurement.

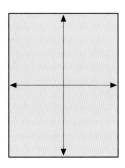

2. Cut or piece corner squares the same width as the borders, including seam allowances.

3. Join the side border strips to the quilt top. Press seams toward the borders.

4. Join a corner square to each end of the top and bottom strips. Press seams toward the border strips. Then join the strips to the top and bottom of the quilt.

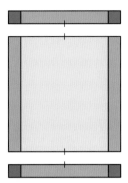

Mitered Borders

1. Estimate the *finished* outside dimensions of your quilt, including borders. Cut four border strips to that length plus 2" to 3". If your quilt is to have multiple borders, join the individual border strips along the lengthwise edges with center points matching, and treat the resulting unit as a single border.

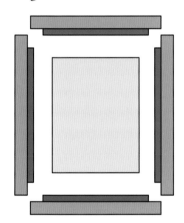

2. Mark ¼" seam intersections on all four corners of the quilt top. Mark the center of each side.

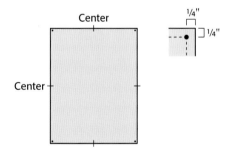

3. Mark the center of each border strip. Measure the distance between the corner marks at the top and bottom of the quilt top and mark the measured distance on the inner edges of two border strips, keeping the center mark at the center. Repeat for the sides.

4. With right sides together, lay the border strips on the quilt top, matching the center and corner marks. Stitch from corner mark to corner mark and no farther. Do not backstitch in case you need to remove a stitch or two. The stitching lines must meet exactly at the corners. Repeat with the remaining border strips.

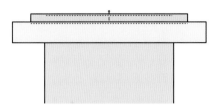

5. With right sides together, fold the quilt diagonally so that the border strips are aligned. Using a right angle or quilter's ruler marked with a 45° angle, draw a line on the wrong side of the top border strip, from the corner mark to the outer edge as shown.

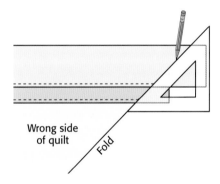

6. Secure the borders with pins and stitch on the drawn line. Make sure the seam is flat and accurate. Then trim the seam allowances to ¼". Press open. Repeat at the remaining corners.

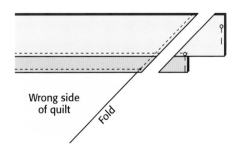

PREPARING TO QUILT

Once your quilt top is complete, you are ready to assemble the layers. Now is the time to press your quilt top well and trim stray threads.

Marking the Quilting Lines

Whether or not to mark the quilting designs depends upon the type of quilting you will be doing. Marking is not necessary if you plan to quilt in the ditch, outline-quilt a uniform distance from seam lines, or free-motion quilt in a random pattern. For more complex designs, you will need to mark the quilt top.

To mark your quilt before the layers are put together:

Use a marking tool that will be visible on your fabric. Test it on scraps from your project first to be sure the marks can be removed easily. To transfer designs, either cut quilting-pattern templates or stencils from plastic or cardboard and draw around them, or place a drawn pattern and the quilt top on a light box or window and trace.

To mark your quilt after the layers are put together:

Use chalk or masking tape to mark quilting designs right before you stitch. Do not leave masking tape on the quilt top any longer than necessary, because it can leave marks.

PREPARING THE QUILT SANDWICH

Layering the quilt top with batting and backing makes the quilt "sandwich." You need to baste these layers together before you quilt.

Backing fabric of a solid color will accent the quilting. A small-scale print with several colors will help hide the quilting stitches and allow you to blend several colors of quilting thread. Beginning quilters may like the way a print forgives a few errors. I prefer a printed back for this reason, and also because I can use pretty fabric.

In this book, the yardage requirements for backings are based on 42"-wide fabric. Backings for quilts that finish wider than 40" must be pieced. If you prefer unpieced backings, purchase 60"-, 90"-, or 108"-wide fabric.

In general, cut or assemble a quilt backing that is at least 2" larger than your quilt top on all sides. On pieced backings, press seams open to make quilting easier.

To assemble the quilt sandwich, spread the quilt backing on the floor or on a large table, wrong side down. To help keep the layers wrinkle-free, you can tape the backing to the work surface. Cover it with batting, and then center the quilt top on the batting. Smooth the top so that it lies flat.

Baste with safety pins, or baste with thread if you are hand quilting. Place the pins 4" to 6" apart and try to avoid areas that will get direct quilting. Remove the pins as needed when you are quilting.

As another option, you can use a fusible batting. When you press the quilt sandwich, the batting bonds to the back and top to help prevent the layers from shifting and wrinkling.

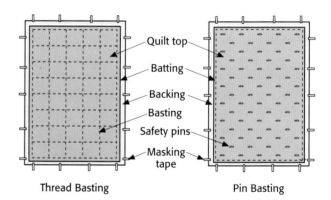

Quilt top
Batting
Backing
Basting
Safety pins
Masking tape

Thread Basting   Pin Basting

QUILTING

The texture that quilting adds to the top really ices the cake. Beautiful quilting patterns in thread work help soften the top and tie the design together.

Machine Quilting

Machine quilting can take your fast-forward quilt to the finish line with beautiful results. If you prefer to piece only and not to do the quilting, your local quilt shop often can give you names of good machine quilters in your area.

Machine quilting is an art that can be mastered with practice. By the end of quilting one quilt, you will have quite a bit of practice. You can quickly fast-forward a small, one-block quilt to use for practice. It is good to use a practice piece to check tension and stitch length with the thread and pattern you plan to use. Set up your sewing machine with plenty of clear table space beside and behind it. If the quilt is large, it will have to be rolled or folded neatly to fit under the machine. Wind several bobbins in advance. Then take a deep breath and begin, stitching four stitches in place to lock the stitching.

Quilting straight lines is perhaps the easiest way to quilt, especially for beginners. For straight-line quilting, it is extremely helpful to have a walking foot to help evenly feed the quilt layers through the machine without shifting or puckering. Some machines have a built-in walking foot while other machines require a separate attachment. A guide bar inserted into your walking foot allows you to stitch evenly spaced lines by using a previous stitching or seam line as a guide.

Walking Foot

For free-motion quilting, you will need a darning foot and the ability to drop the feed dogs on your machine. With free-motion quilting, you guide the fabric in the direction of the design rather than turn the fabric under the needle. You determine the stitch length by keeping a balance between the motion of your hands and your foot speed on the pedal. Use a faster foot speed while free-motion quilting than you would use for piecing. This maintains better stitch length and smoother rhythm. The entire process will take some getting used to and may cause some stress as you develop your rhythm. Relax, stop and roll your shoulders, and then continue to let the quilting pattern and rhythm develop.

To end your stitching, whether you've quilted straight lines or tried free-motion quilting, take four stitches in place. See Maurine Noble's book *Machine Quilting Made Easy* (Martingale & Company, 1994), for more information on machine quilting.

Use free-motion quilting to quilt a motif from a stencil and to create an allover fill design like stipple quilting. I like to practice on paper with no thread in my needle when I try a new design. Working from side to side, fill the paper evenly with the design. The following drawings illustrate some of the patterns used in this book.

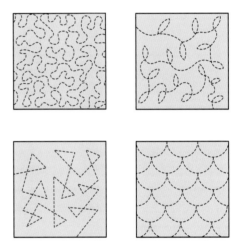

Hand Quilting

Even if you piece with interfacing you can still hand quilt. Lightweight interfacing adds minimal bulk and won't interfere with the beautiful look of handmade stitches. You may notice, however, that the slight bulk reduces the number of stitches you are able to put on the needle at one time.

To quilt by hand, you need short, sturdy needles (called Betweens), quilting thread, and a thimble to fit the middle finger of your sewing hand. Most quilters also use a frame or hoop to support their work. Use the smallest size Between needle that you can comfortably handle: the finer the needle, the smaller your stitches will be.

Pulling the needle through the seam allowances can be difficult, so plan your quilting design to avoid areas where pieces intersect. Choose a high-quality, strong Between needle that will withstand the quilting stitch without bending. At the beginning of a quilting session, thread several needles with 18" lengths of thread so that you won't have to frequently stop and re-thread.

1. Begin quilting with a knotted thread. Insert the needle through the top layer of the quilt about 1" from the point where you want to start stitching. Slide the needle through the batting and bring the needle out at the starting point. Gently tug on the thread until the knot pops through the fabric and is buried in the batting.

2. Take a backstitch and begin quilting. Insert the needle vertically until it touches the finger beneath the quilt. Then rock the needle upward to make a small stitch. Repeat for several stitches before pulling the thread through. Use the thimble to protect the finger pushing the needle through. Consider wearing a rubber fingertip on your index finger to help you grip the needle as you pull it through.

3. To end your stitches, make a single knot about ¼" from the quilt top. Take one backstitch into the quilt and tug on the knot until it pops into the batting. Bring the needle out ¾" away from your last stitch and clip the thread.

Hand-Quilting Stitch

ADDING A HANGING SLEEVE

To display your quilt on a wall, add a hanging sleeve to the back of the quilt. Use a scrap of backing material for a sleeve that blends well. Slip a rod, dowel, or wooden slat through the sleeve to hang the quilt.

1. Cut an 8½"-wide strip of fabric as long as the width of the quilt. Hem both short ends of the strip so that the sleeve is about 1" shorter than the quilt on both ends.

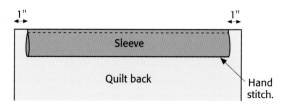

2. Fold the strip wrong sides together and pin the raw edges to the top of the quilt before you attach the binding. Baste ⅛" from the edge. Sew the binding to the quilt as described below.

3. Blindstitch the folded edge of the sleeve to the back of your quilt.

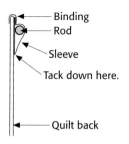

BINDING

Double-fold binding adds a durable finishing touch to your quilt. All projects in this book are finished with a 2½"-wide, straight-grain binding. To cut binding strips, cut across the width of the fabric from selvage to selvage. Then join the strips to form a continuous length.

To determine the number of binding strips needed, measure the four edges of the quilt. Add the measurements, and then add 10" to that number to allow for joining the strips. Divide this number by 40" and you'll know how many strips to cut.

Prepare the quilt for binding by removing any safety pins or thread you used for basting the quilt layers and lightly press the hanging sleeve in place. To allow the layers to feed evenly through the machine, use a walking foot when you apply the binding.

1. Cut the number of 2½"-wide strips needed. Lay the first strip right side up. Lay the second strip, wrong side up, across the first strip at a right angle. Imagine that the two strips are hands on a clock pointing to 9 o'clock (right side up) and 6 o'clock (wrong side up). Stitch diagonally across the end of the strips.

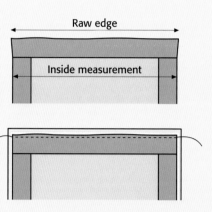

Raw edge

Inside measurement

> ➤➤ TIP: Are your borders wavy? On the outside border, if the raw edge measurement is now longer than the quilt edge to which it was sewn, you'll have a wavy outside edge. This may be due to unequal amounts of quilting, poor measurements, or gremlins! Correct this prior to binding the quilt by hand stitching a long basting stitch ⅛" away from the raw edge of the border through all three layers. Gently gather and ease in the fullness.

2. Continue joining the strips to make the length required. Trim the excess and press the seam allowances open.

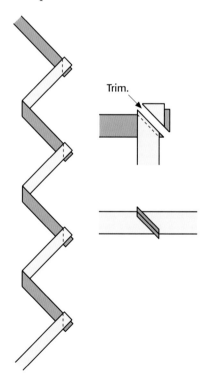

Trim.

3. Fold the strip in half lengthwise, wrong sides together, and press.

4. Lay the binding along the lower-left portion of the quilt—not at a corner—and align the raw edges of the binding with the quilt top. Using a ¼" seam allowance, begin stitching 6" from the end of the strip.

5. Stop stitching ¼" from the corner. With the needle down, pivot and stitch diagonally to the corner.

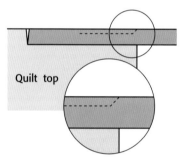

Quilt top

6. Turn the quilt to sew the next side. Fold the binding strip up toward the 12 o'clock position and then down. The fold should line up with the top edge of the quilt, and the raw edges should be even with the side to be stitched. Stitch from the edge to the next corner. Stop ¼" away from the edge, pivot, and stitch diagonally to the corner. Repeat the corner fold. Continue for the remaining corners.

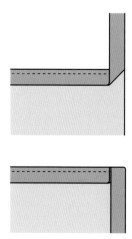

7. After the last corner is stitched, stop. Overlap the ends of the binding. Make a ⅛"-deep clip through all four binding layers. Be careful not to cut the quilt.

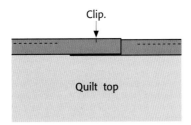

8. Open the folded strips. Lay the ending binding strip right side up. Lay the beginning binding strip, wrong side up, across the ending strip at a right angle. Imagine that the two strips are hands on a clock pointing to 9 o'clock (right side up) and 6 o'clock (wrong side up). Use the clips to align the left and top edges of the binding strips as shown. Pin the strips.

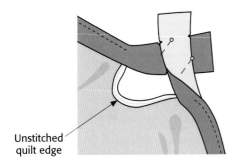

9. Stitch diagonally across the end of the strips. Make certain that the joined binding fits, and then trim the excess fabric to ¼". Press the seam allowance open.

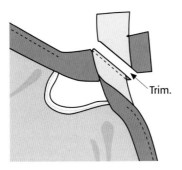

10. Refold the seamed section and align it with the quilt edge. Complete the stitching.

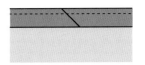

11. Trim the batting and backing even with the raw edges of the binding. Fold the binding to the back, over the raw edges of the quilt. The folded edge of the binding should cover the machine stitching. Hand stitch or machine stitch the binding in place, mitering the corners.

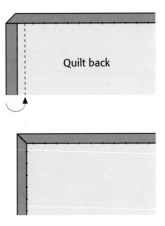

SIGNING YOUR QUILT

Be sure to sign and date your quilt. Labels can be very elaborate or simple. Include the name of the quilt, your name, the city and state where the quilt was completed, the date, the name of the recipient if it is a gift, and any other interesting or important information about the quilt. Include the name of the quilter as well if you had someone else quilt the top for you.